PROCEDURES FOR

PORT STATE CONTROL

*Resolution A.787(19), as amended
by resolution A.882(21)*

2000 Edition

INTERNATIONAL
MARITIME
ORGANIZATION

London, 2001

First published in 2001 by the
INTERNATIONAL MARITIME ORGANIZATION
4 Albert Embankment, London SE1 7SR

www.imo.org

Printed in the United Kingdom by CPI Books Limited, Reading RG1 8EX

ISBN: 978-92-801-5099-5

IMO PUBLICATION
Sales number: IA650E

This publication has been prepared from official documents of IMO, and every effort has been made to
eliminate errors and reproduce the original text(s) faithfully. Readers should be aware that,
in case of inconsistency, the official IMO text will prevail.

020224

Foreword

Port State control (PSC) has become of ever increasing importance in the field of maritime safety and marine pollution prevention and thus in the work of the International Maritime Organization over the past few years.

Since the adoption in 1981 of Assembly resolution A.466(XII) on Procedures for the Control of Ships, a number of resolutions relating to PSC have been adopted.

The IMO Sub-Committee on Flag State Implementation (FSI), recognizing the need for a single comprehensive document to facilitate the work of maritime administrations in general and PSC inspectors in particular, reviewed and amalgamated existing resolutions and documents on PSC. This resulted in the adoption, by the nineteenth IMO Assembly in 1995, of resolution A.787(19) on Procedures for Port State Control.

The resolution provides basic guidance to Port State Control Officers (PSCOs) on the conduct of PSC inspections, in order to promote consistency in the conduct of inspections worldwide, and harmonize the criteria for deciding on deficiencies of a ship, its equipment and its crew, as well as the application of control procedures.

In adopting the resolution, the Assembly requested the MSC and the MEPC to continue their work on PSC with a view to improving the above Procedures as and when the need arises, on the basis of the experience gained in their implementation.

Developments in the intervening period, including amendments to IMO instruments referred to in the Procedures, prompted proposals for amendments to resolution A.787(19). These include the incorporation of additional guidelines for PSC related to the ISM Code and for PSC under the 1969 Tonnage Convention, provisions on suspension of inspections, procedures for the rectification of deficiencies and release, updating of reporting formats and of the list of certificates and documents to be checked during inspections and other changes. The relevant amendments were prepared by the FSI Sub-Committee at its seventh session, approved by MSC and MEPC at their seventy-first and forty-third session respectively and adopted by the twenty-first Assembly in November 1999 as Assembly resolution A.882(21) on Amendments to the Procedures for Port State Control.

With a view to facilitating the work of Administrations and in particular the work of PSCOs in the field by making an updated text of the Procedures available, this publication contains the consolidated text of

iii

resolution A.787(19), incorporating the amendments adopted by resolution A.882(21). To assist PSCOs in the fulfilment of their reporting obligations it also includes, in appendix 10, updated information on contact addresses of responsible national authorities.

Contents

v

Chapter 1
General

1.1 Purpose

This document is intended to provide basic guidance on the conduct of port State control inspections and afford consistency in the conduct of these inspections, the recognition of deficiencies of a ship, its equipment or its crew, and the application of control procedures.

1.2 Application

1.2.1 The procedures apply to ships which come under the provisions of the International Convention for the Safety of Life at Sea, 1974, as amended (SOLAS 74), the Protocol of 1988 relating to the International Convention for the Safety of Life at Sea, 1974 (SOLAS Protocol 1988), the International Convention on Load Lines, 1966 (Load Lines 66), the Protocol of 1988 relating to the International Convention on Load Lines, 1966 (Load Line Protocol 88), the International Convention for the Prevention of Pollution from Ships, 1973 as modified by the Protocol of 1978 relating thereto, as amended (MARPOL 73/78), the International Convention on Standards of Training, Certification and Watchkeeping for Seafarers, 1978, as amended (STCW 78), and the International Convention on Tonnage Measurement of Ships, 1969 (Tonnage 69), hereafter referred to as the applicable conventions.

1.2.2 Ships of non-parties or below convention size shall be given no more favourable treatment (see section 1.5).

1.2.3 In exercising port State control, Parties will only apply those provisions of the conventions which are in force and which they have accepted.

1.2.4 If a port State exercises port State control based on International Labour Organization (ILO) Convention No.147, "Merchant Shipping (Minimum Standards) Convention, 1976", guidance on the conduct of such control inspections is given in the ILO publication *Inspection of Labour Conditions on Board Ship: Guidelines for Procedure.*

1.3 Introduction

1.3.1 Under the provisions of the applicable conventions listed in section 1.2 above, the Administration (i.e. the Government of the flag State) is responsible for promulgating laws and regulations and for taking all other steps which may be necessary to give the applicable conventions full and complete effect so as to ensure that, from the point of view of safety of life and pollution prevention, a ship is fit for the service for which it is intended and seafarers are qualified and fit for their duties.

1.3.2 In some cases it may be difficult for the Administration to exercise full and continuous control over some ships entitled to fly the flag of its State, for instance those ships which do not regularly call at a port of the flag State. The problem can be, and has been, partly overcome by appointing inspectors at foreign ports and/or authorizing recognized organizations to act on behalf of the flag State Administration.

1.3.3 The following control procedures should be regarded as complementary to national measures taken by Administrations of flag States in their countries and abroad and are intended to provide assistance to flag State Administrations in securing compliance with convention provisions in safeguarding the safety of crew, passengers and ships, and ensuring the prevention of pollution.

1.4   Provision for port State control

Regulation 19 of chapter I of SOLAS 74, as modified by the SOLAS Protocol 88, regulation 6.2 of chapter IX and regulation 4 of chapter XI of SOLAS 74; article 21 of Load Lines 66, as modified by the Load Line Protocol 88; articles 5 and 6, regulation 8A of Annex I, regulation 15 of Annex II, regulation 8 of Annex III and regulation 8 of Annex V of MARPOL 73/78; article X of STCW 78; and article 12 of Tonnage 69 provide for control procedures to be followed by a Party to a relevant convention with regard to foreign ships visiting their ports. The authorities of port States should make effective use of these provisions for the purposes of identifying deficiencies, if any, in such ships which may render them substandard (see section 4.1), and ensuring that remedial measures are taken.

1.5   Ships of non-Parties and ships below convention size

1.5.1 Article II(3) of the Protocol of 1978 to SOLAS 74, article 5(4) of MARPOL 73/78, and article X(5) of STCW 78 provide that no more favourable treatment is to be given to the ships of countries which are not Party to the Convention. All Parties should as a matter of principle apply the procedures set out in this document to ships of non-parties and ships below convention size in order to ensure that equivalent surveys and inspections are conducted and an equivalent level of safety and protection of the marine environment are ensured.

1.5.2 As ships of non-parties and ships below convention size are not provided with SOLAS, Load Line or MARPOL certificates, as applicable, or the crew members may not hold valid STCW certificates, the Port State Control Officer (PSCO), taking into account the principles established in this document, should be satisfied that the ship and crew do not present a danger to those on board or an unreasonable threat of harm to the marine environment. If the ship or crew has some form of certification other than that required by a convention, the PSCO may take the form and content of this documentation into account in the evaluation of that ship. The conditions of and on such a ship and its equipment and the certification of the crew and the flag State's minimum manning standards should be compatible with the aims of the provisions of the conventions; otherwise, the ship should be subject to such restrictions as are necessary to obtain a comparable level of safety and protection of the marine environment.

1.6 Definitions

1.6.1 *Clear grounds:* Evidence that the ship, its equipment, or its crew does not correspond substantially with the requirements of the relevant conventions or that the master or crew members are not familiar with essential shipboard procedures relating to the safety of ships or the prevention of pollution. Examples of clear grounds are included in section 2.3.

1.6.2 *Deficiency:* A condition found not to be in compliance with the requirements of the relevant convention.

1.6.3 *Detention:* Intervention action taken by the port State when the condition of the ship or its crew does not correspond substantially with the applicable conventions to ensure that the ship will not sail until it can proceed to sea without presenting a danger to the ship or persons on board, or without presenting an unreasonable threat of harm to the marine environment, whether or not such action will affect the normal schedule of the departure of the ship.

1.6.4 *Inspection:* A visit on board a ship to check both the validity of the relevant certificates and other documents, and the overall condition of the ship, its equipment, and its crew.

1.6.5 *More detailed inspection:* An inspection conducted when there are clear grounds for believing that the condition of the ship, its equipment, or its crew does not correspond substantially with the particulars of the certificates.

1.6.6 *Port State Control Officer (PSCO):* A person duly authorized by the competent authority of a Party to a relevant convention to carry out port State control inspections, and responsible exclusively to that Party.

1.6.7 *Recognized organization:* An organization which meets the relevant conditions set forth by resolution A.739(18), and has been delegated by the flag State Administration to provide the necessary statutory services and certification to ships entitled to fly its flag.

1.6.8 *Stoppage of an operation:* Formal prohibition against a ship to continue an operation due to an identified deficiency(ies) which, singly or together, render the continuation of such operation hazardous.

1.6.9 *Substandard ship:* A ship whose hull, machinery, equipment, or operational safety is substantially below the standards required by the relevant convention or whose crew is not in conformance with the safe manning document.

1.6.10 *Valid certificates:* A certificate that has been issued directly by a Party to a relevant convention or on its behalf by a recognized organization and contains accurate and effective dates, meets the provisions of the relevant convention and with which the particulars of the ship, its crew and its equipment correspond.

Chapter 2
Port State inspections

2.1 General

2.1.1 In accordance with the provisions of the applicable conventions, Parties may conduct inspections by PSCOs of foreign ships in their ports.

2.1.2 Such inspections may be undertaken on the basis of:

.1 the initiative of the Party;

.2 the request of, or on the basis of, information regarding a ship provided by another Party; or

.3 information regarding a ship provided by a member of the crew, a professional body, an association, a trade union or any other individual with an interest in the safety of the ship, its crew and passengers, or the protection of the marine environment.

2.1.3 Whereas Parties may entrust surveys and inspections of ships entitled to fly their own flag either to inspectors nominated for this purpose or to recognized organizations, they should be made aware that, under the applicable conventions, foreign ships are subject to port State control, including boarding, inspection, remedial action, and possible detention, only by officers duly authorized by the port State. This authorization of PSCOs may be a general grant of authority or may be specific on a case-by-case basis.

2.1.4 All possible efforts should be made to avoid a ship being unduly detained or delayed. If a ship is unduly detained or delayed, it should be entitled to compensation for any loss or damage suffered.

2.2 Inspections

2.2.1 In the pursuance of control procedures under the applicable conventions, which, for instance, may arise from information given to a port State regarding a ship, a PSCO may proceed to the ship and before boarding gain, from its appearance in the water, an impression of its standard of maintenance from such items as the condition of its paintwork, corrosion or pitting or unrepaired damage.

2.2.2 At the earliest possible opportunity the PSCO should ascertain the year of build and size of the ship for the purpose of determining which provisions of the conventions are applicable.

2.2.3 On boarding and introduction to the master or the responsible ship's officer, the PSCO should examine the vessel's relevant certificates and documents, as listed in appendix 4. When examining 1969 International Tonnage Certificates, the PSCO should be guided by appendix 4A.

2.2.4 If the certificates are valid and the PSCO's general impression and visual observations on board confirm a good standard of maintenance, the PSCO should generally confine the inspection to reported or observed deficiencies, if any.

2.2.5 If, however, the PSCO from general impressions or observations on board has clear grounds for believing that the ship, its equipment or its crew do not substantially meet the requirements, the PSCO should proceed to a more detailed inspection, taking into consideration chapter 3.

2.2.6 In pursuance of control procedures under chapter IX of SOLAS 74 on the International Management Code for the Safe Operation of Ships and for Pollution Prevention (ISM Code), the PSCO should utilize the guidelines in section 3.7.

2.3   Clear grounds

"Clear grounds" to conduct a more detailed inspection include:

.1   the absence of principal equipment or arrangements required by the conventions;

.2   evidence from a review of the ship's certificates that a certificate or certificates are clearly invalid;

.3   evidence that documentation required by the conventions and listed in appendix 4 are not on board, incomplete, are not maintained or are falsely maintained;

.4   evidence from the PSCO's general impressions and observations that serious hull or structural deterioration or deficiencies exist that may place at risk the structural, watertight or weathertight integrity of the ship;

.5   evidence from the PSCO's general impressions or observations that serious deficiencies exist in the safety, pollution prevention or navigational equipment;

.6   information or evidence that the master or crew is not familiar with essential shipboard operations relating to the safety of ships or the prevention of pollution, or that such operations have not been carried out;

.7   indications that key crew members may not be able to communicate with each other or with other persons on board;

.8   the emission of false distress alerts not followed by proper cancellation procedures;

.9   receipt of a report or complaint containing information that a ship appears to be substandard.

2.4   Professional profile of PSCOs

2.4.1 Port State control should be carried out only by qualified PSCOs who fulfil the criteria specified in section 2.5.

2.4.2 When the required professional expertise cannot be provided by the PSCO, the PSCO may be assisted by any person with the required expertise acceptable to the port State.

2.4.3 The PSCOs and the persons assisting them should have no commercial interest, either in the port of inspection or in the ships inspected, nor should PSCOs be employed by or undertake work on behalf of recognized organizations.

2.4.4 A PSCO should carry a personal document in the form of an identity card issued by the port State and indicating that the PSCO is authorized to carry out the control.

2.5   Qualification and training requirements of PSCOs

2.5.1 The PSCO should be an experienced officer qualified as flag State surveyor.

2.5.2 The PSCO should be able to communicate in English with the key crew.

2.5.3 Training should be provided for PSCOs to give the necessary knowledge of the provisions of the applicable conventions which are relevant to the conduct of port State control, taking into account the latest IMO Model Courses for port State control.

2.5.4 In specifying the qualifications and training requirements for PSCOs, the Administration should take into account, as appropriate, which of the internationally agreed instruments are relevant for the control by the port State and the variety of types of ships which may enter its ports.

2.5.5 PSCOs carrying out inspections of operational requirements should be qualified as: a master or chief engineer and have appropriate seagoing experience, or have qualifications from an institution recognized by the Administration in a maritime related field and have specialized training to ensure adequate competence and skill, or be a qualified officer of the Administration with an equivalent level of experience and training, for performing inspections of the relevant operational requirements.

2.5.6 Periodical seminars for PSCOs should be held in order to update their knowledge with respect to instruments related to port State control.

2.6 General procedural guidelines for PSCOs

2.6.1 The PSCO should use professional judgement in carrying out all duties, and consider consulting others as deemed appropriate.

2.6.2 When boarding a ship, the PSCO should present to the master or to the representative of the owner, if requested to do so, the PSCO identity card. This card should be accepted as documented evidence that the PSCO in question is duly authorized by the Administration to carry out port State control inspections.

2.6.3 If the PSCO has clear grounds for carrying out a more detailed inspection, the master should be immediately informed of these grounds and advised that, if so desired, the master may contact the Administration or, as appropriate, the recognized organization responsible for issuing the relevant certificate and invite their presence on board.

2.6.4 In the case that an inspection is initiated based on a report or complaint, especially if it is from a crew member, the source of the information should not be disclosed.

2.6.5 When exercising control, all possible efforts should be made to avoid a ship being unduly detained or delayed. It should be borne in mind that the main purpose of port State control is to prevent a ship proceeding to sea if it is unsafe or presents an unreasonable threat of harm to the marine environment. The PSCO should exercise professional judgement to determine whether to detain a ship until the deficiencies are corrected or to allow it to sail with certain deficiencies, having regard to the particular circumstances of the intended voyage.

2.6.6 It should be recognized that all equipment is subject to failure and spares or replacement parts may not be readily available. In such cases, undue delay should not be caused if, in the opinion of the PSCO, safe alternative arrangements have been made.

2.6.7 Where the grounds for detention are the result of accidental damage suffered on the ship's voyage to a port, no detention order should be issued, provided that:

.1   due account has been given to the convention requirements regarding notification to the flag State Administration, the nominated surveyor or the recognized organization responsible for issuing the relevant certificate;

.2   prior to entering a port, the master or company has submitted to the port State authority details on the circumstances of the accident and the damage suffered and information about the required notification of the flag State Administration;

.3   appropriate remedial action, to the satisfaction of the port State authority, is being taken by the ship; and

.4   the port State authority has ensured, having been notified of the completion of the remedial action, that deficiencies which were clearly hazardous to safety, health or environment have been rectified.

2.6.8 Since detention of a ship is a serious matter involving many issues, it may be in the best interest of the PSCO to act with other interested parties. For example, the officer may request the owner's representatives to provide proposals for correcting the situation. The PSCO may also consider co-operating with the flag State Administration's representatives or recognized organization responsible for issuing the relevant certificates, and consulting them regarding their acceptance of the owner's proposals and their possible additional requirements. Without limiting the PSCO's discretion in any way, the involvement of other parties could result in a safer ship, avoid subsequent arguments relating to the circumstances of the detention and prove advantageous in the case of litigation involving "undue delay".

2.6.9 Where deficiencies cannot be remedied at the port of inspection, the PSCO may allow the ship to proceed to another port, subject to any appropriate conditions determined. In such circumstances, the PSCO should ensure that the competent authority of the next port of call and the flag State are notified.

2.6.10 Detention reports to the flag State should be in sufficient detail for an assessment to be made of the severity of the deficiencies giving rise to the detention.

2.6.11 The company or its representative have a right of appeal against a detention taken by the authority of a port State. The appeal should not cause the detention to be suspended. The PSCO should properly inform the master of the right of appeal.

2.6.12   To ensure consistent enforcement of port State control require-ments, PSCOs should carry an extract of section 2.6 (General Procedural Guidelines for PSCOs) for ready reference when carrying out any port State control inspections.

Chapter 3
More detailed inspections

3.1   General

3.1.1 If the ship does not carry valid certificates, or if the PSCO, from general impressions or observations on board, has clear grounds for believing that the condition of the ship or its equipment does not correspond substantially with the particulars of the certificates or that the master or crew is not familiar with essential shipboard procedures, a more detailed inspection as described in this chapter should be carried out.

3.1.2 It is not envisaged that all of the equipment and procedures outlined in this chapter would be checked during a single port State control inspection, unless the condition of the ship or the familiarity of the master or crew with essential shipboard procedures necessitates such a detailed inspection. In addition, these guidelines are not intended to impose the seafarer certification programme of the port State on a ship entitled to fly the flag of another Party to STCW 78 or to impose control procedures on foreign ships in excess of those imposed on ships of the port State.

3.2   Clear grounds

When a PSCO inspects a foreign ship which is required to hold a convention certificate, and which is in a port or an offshore terminal under the jurisdiction of that State, any such inspection should be limited to verifying that there are on board valid certificates and other relevant documentation and to the PSCO forming an impression of the overall condition of the ship, its equipment and its crew, unless there are "clear grounds" for believing that the condition of the ship or its equipment does not correspond substantially with the particulars of the certificates.

3.3   Guidelines for ship structural and equipment requirements

3.3.1 If the PSCO, from general impressions or observations on board, has clear grounds for believing that the ship might be substandard, the PSCO should proceed to a more detailed inspection, taking the following considerations into account.

Structure

3.3.2 The PSCO's impression of hull maintenance and the general state on deck, the condition of such items as ladderways, guard-rails, pipe

11

coverings and areas of corrosion or pitting should influence the PSCO's decision as to whether it is necessary to make the fullest possible examination of the structure with the ship afloat. Significant areas of damage or corrosion, or pitting of plating and associated stiffening in decks and hull affecting seaworthiness or strength to take local loads, may justify detention. It may be necessary for the underwater portion of the ship to be checked. In reaching a decision, the PSCO should have regard to the seaworthiness and not the age of the ship, making an allowance for fair wear and tear over the minimum acceptable scantlings. Damage not affecting seaworthiness will not constitute grounds for judging that a ship should be detained, nor will damage that has been temporarily but effectively repaired for a voyage to a port for permanent repairs. However, in this assessment of the effect of damage, the PSCO should have regard to the location of crew accommodation and whether the damage substantially affects its habitability.

3.3.3 The PSCO should pay particular attention to the structural integrity and seaworthiness of bulk carriers and oil tankers and note that these ships must undergo the enhanced programme of inspection during surveys under the provision of regulation XI/2 of SOLAS 74.

3.3.4 The PSCO's assessment of the safety of the structure of those ships should be based on the Survey Report File carried on board. This file should contain reports of structural surveys, condition evaluation reports (translated into English and endorsed by or on behalf of the Administration), thickness measurement reports and a survey planning document. The PSCO should note that there may be a short delay in the update of the Survey Report File following survey. Where there is doubt that the required survey has taken place, the PSCO should seek confirmation from the recognized organization.

3.3.5 If the Survey Report File necessitates a more detailed inspection of the structure of the ship or if no such report is carried, special attention should be given by the PSCO, as appropriate, to hull structure, piping systems in way of cargo tanks or holds, pump-rooms, cofferdams, pipe tunnels, void spaces within the cargo area and ballast tanks.

3.3.6 For bulk carriers, PSCOs should inspect the main structure of holds for any obviously unauthorized repairs.

Machinery spaces

3.3.7 The PSCO should assess the condition of the machinery and of the electrical installations to make sure that they are capable of providing sufficient continuous power for propulsion and for auxiliary services.

3.3.8 During inspection of the machinery spaces the PSCO should form an impression of the standard of maintenance. Frayed or disconnected quick-closing valve wires, disconnected or inoperative extended control rods or machinery trip mechanisms, missing valve hand wheels, evidence of chronic steam, water and oil leaks, dirty tank tops and bilges or extensive corrosion of machinery foundations are pointers to an unsatisfactory organization of the systems' maintenance. A large number of temporary repairs, including pipe clips or cement boxes, will indicate reluctance to make permanent repairs.

3.3.9 While it is not possible to determine the condition of the machinery without performance trials, general deficiencies, such as leaking pump glands, dirty water gauge glasses, inoperable pressure gauges, rusted relief valves, inoperative or disconnected safety or control devices, evidence of repeated operation of diesel engine scavenge belt or crankcase relief valves, malfunctioning or inoperative automatic equipment and alarm systems and leaking boiler casings or uptakes, would warrant inspection of the engine-room log-book and investigation into the record of machinery failures and accidents and a request for running tests of machinery.

3.3.10 If one electrical generator is out of commission, the PSCO should investigate whether power is available to maintain essential and emergency services and should conduct tests.

3.3.11 If evidence of neglect becomes evident, the PSCO should extend the scope of an investigation to include, for example, tests on the main and auxiliary steering gear arrangements, overspeed trips, circuit breakers, etc.

3.3.12 It must be stressed that while detection of one or more of the above deficiencies would afford guidance to a substandard condition, the actual combination is a matter for professional judgement in each case.

Conditions of assignment of load lines

3.3.13 It may be that the PSCO has concluded that a hull inspection is unnecessary but, if dissatisfied, on the basis of observations on deck, with items such as defective hatch closing arrangements, corroded air pipes and vent coamings, the PSCO should examine closely the conditions of assignment of load lines, paying particular attention to closing appliances, means of freeing water from the deck and arrangements concerned with the protection of the crew.

Life-saving appliances

3.3.14 The effectiveness of life-saving appliances depends heavily on good maintenance by the crew and their use in regular drills. The lapse of time

13

since the last survey for a Safety Equipment Certificate can be a significant factor in the degree of deterioration of equipment if it has not been subject to regular inspection by the crew. Apart from failure to carry equipment required by a convention or obvious defects such as holed lifeboats, the PSCO should look for signs of disuse of, or obstructions to, survival craft launching equipment which may include paint accumulation, seizing of pivot points, absence of greasing, condition of blocks and falls and improper lashing or stowing of deck cargo.

3.3.15 Should such signs be evident, the PSCO would be justified in making a detailed inspection of all life-saving appliances. Such an examination might include the lowering of survival craft, a check on the servicing of liferafts, the number and condition of lifejackets and lifebuoys and ensuring that the pyrotechnics are still within their period of validity. It would not normally be as detailed as that for a renewal of the Safety Equipment Certificate and would concentrate on essentials for safe abandonment of the ship, but in an extreme case could progress to a full Safety Equipment Certificate inspection. The provision and functioning of effective overside lighting, means of alerting the crew and passengers and provision of illuminated routes to assembly points and embarkation positions should be given importance in the inspection.

Fire safety

3.3.16 Ships in general: the poor condition of fire and wash deck lines and hydrants and the possible absence of fire hoses and extinguishers in accommodation spaces might be a guide to a need for a close inspection of all fire safety equipment. In addition to compliance with convention requirements, the PSCO should look for evidence of a higher than normal fire risk; this might be brought about by a poor standard of cleanliness in the machinery space, which together with significant deficiencies of fixed or portable fire-extinguishing equipment could lead to a judgement of the ship being substandard.

3.3.17 Passenger ships: the PSCO should initially form an opinion of the need for inspection of the fire safety arrangements on the basis of consideration of the ship as described in the preceding sections and, in particular, that dealing with fire safety equipment. If the PSCO considers that a more detailed inspection of fire safety arrangements is necessary, the PSCO should examine the fire control plan on board in order to obtain a general picture of the fire safety measures provided on board the ship and consider their compliance with convention requirements for the year of build. Queries on the method of structural protection should be addressed to the flag Administration and the PSCO should generally confine the inspection to the effectiveness of the arrangements provided.

3.3.18 The spread of fire could be accelerated if fire doors are not readily operable. The PSCO should inspect for the operability and securing arrangements of those doors in the main zone bulkheads and stairway enclosures and in boundaries of high fire risk spaces, such as main machinery rooms and galleys, giving particular attention to those retained in the open position. Attention should also be given to main vertical zones which may have been compromised through new construction. An additional hazard in the event of fire is the spread of smoke through ventilation systems. Spot checks might be made on dampers and smoke flaps to ascertain the standard of operability. The PSCO should also ensure that ventilation fans can be stopped from the master controls and that means are available for closing main inlets and outlets of ventilation systems.

3.3.19 Attention should be given to the effectiveness of escape routes by ensuring that vital doors are not kept locked and that alleyways and stairways are not obstructed.

Regulations for preventing collisions at sea

3.3.20 A vital aspect of ensuring safety of life at sea is full compliance with the collision regulations. Based on observations on deck, the PSCO should consider the need for close inspection of lanterns and their screening and means of making sound and distress signals.

Cargo Ship Safety Construction Certificate

3.3.21 The general condition of the ship may lead the PSCO to consider matters other than those concerned with safety equipment and assignment of load lines, but nevertheless associated with the safety of the vessel, such as the effectiveness of items associated with the Cargo Ship Safety Construction Certificate, which can include pumping arrangements, means for shutting off air and oil supplies in the event of fire, alarm systems and emergency power supplies.

Cargo Ship Safety Radio Certificates

3.3.22 The validity of the Cargo Ship Safety Radio Certificates and associated Record of Equipment (Form R) may be accepted as proof of the provision and effectiveness of its associated equipment, but the PSCO should ensure that appropriate certificated personnel are carried for its operation and for listening periods. Requirements for maintenance of radio equipment are contained in SOLAS regulation IV/15. The radio log or radio records should be examined. Where considered necessary, operational checks may be carried out.

Equipment in excess of convention or flag State requirements

3.3.23 Equipment on board which is expected to be relied on in situations affecting safety or pollution prevention must be in operating condition. If such equipment is inoperative and is in excess of the equipment required by an appropriate convention and/or the flag State, it should be repaired, removed or, if removal is not practicable, clearly marked as inoperative and secured.

3.4 Guidelines for discharge requirements under Annexes I and II of MARPOL 73/78

3.4.1 Regulations 9 and 10 of Annex I of MARPOL 73/78 prohibit the discharge into the sea of oil and regulation 5 of Annex II of MARPOL 73/78 prohibits the discharge into the sea of noxious liquid substances except under precisely defined conditions. A record of these operations should be completed, where appropriate, in the form of an Oil or Cargo Record Book as applicable and should be readily available for inspection at all reasonable times.

3.4.2 The regulations referred to above provide that, whenever visible traces of oil are observed on or below the surface of the water in the immediate vicinity of a ship or of its wake, a Party should, to the extent that it is reasonably able to do so, promptly investigate the facts bearing on the issue of whether or not there has been a violation of the discharge provisions.

3.4.3 The conditions under which noxious liquid substances are permitted to be discharged into the seas include quantity, quality, and position limitations, which depend on the category of substance and the sea area.

3.4.4 An investigation into an alleged contravention should therefore aim to establish whether a noxious liquid substance has been discharged and whether the operations leading to that discharge were in accordance with the ship's Procedures and Arrangements Manual (P and A Manual).

3.4.5 Recognizing the likelihood that many of the violations of the discharge provisions will take place outside the immediate control and knowledge of the flag State, article 6 of MARPOL 73/78 provides that Parties shall co-operate in the detection of violations and the enforcement of the provisions using all appropriate and practicable measures of detection and environmental monitoring, adequate procedures for reporting and gathering evidence. MARPOL 73/78 also contains a number of more specific provisions designed to facilitate that co-operation.

3.4.6 Several sources of information about possible violations of the discharge provisions can be indicated. These include:

.1 reports by masters: article 8 and Protocol I of MARPOL 73/78 require *inter alia* a ship's master to report certain incidents involving the discharge or the probability of a discharge of oil or oily mixtures, or noxious liquid substances or mixtures containing such substances;

.2 reports by official bodies: article 8 of MARPOL 73/78 requires furthermore that a Party issue instructions to its maritime inspection vessels and aircraft and to other appropriate services to report to its authorities incidents involving the discharge or the probability of a discharge of oil or oily mixtures, or noxious liquid substances or mixtures containing such substances;

.3 reports by other Parties: article 6 of MARPOL 73/78 provides that a Party may request another Party to inspect a ship. The Party making the request shall supply sufficient evidence that the ship has discharged oil or oily mixtures, noxious liquid substances or mixtures containing such substances, or that the ship has departed from the unloading port with residues of noxious liquid substances in excess of those permitted to be discharged into the sea;

.4 reports by others: It is not possible to list exhaustively all sources of information concerning alleged contravention of the discharge provisions. Parties should take all circumstances into account when deciding upon investigating such reports.

3.4.7 Action which can be taken by States other than the flag or port States that have information on discharge violations (hereinafter referred to as coastal States):

.1 Coastal States, which are Parties to MARPOL 73/78, upon receiving a report of pollution by oil or noxious liquid substances allegedly caused by a ship, may investigate the matter and collect such evidence as can be collected. For details of the desired evidence, reference is made to appendices 2 and 3.

.2 If the investigation referred to under .1 above discloses that the next port of call of the ship in question lies within its jurisdiction, the coastal State should also take port State action as set out in paragraphs 3.4.8 to 3.4.13 below.

.3 If the investigation referred to in .1 above discloses that the next port of call of the ship in question lies within the jurisdiction of another Party, then the coastal State should in appropriate cases furnish the evidence to that other Party and request that Party to take port State action in accordance with paragraphs 3.4.8 to 3.4.13 below.

.4 In either case referred to in .2 and .3 above and if the next port of call of the ship in question cannot be ascertained, the coastal State shall inform the flag State of the incident and of the evidence obtained.

Port State action

3.4.8 Parties shall appoint or authorize officers to carry out investigations for the purpose of verifying whether a ship has discharged oil or noxious liquid substances in violation of the provisions of MARPOL 73/78.

3.4.9 Parties may undertake such investigations on the basis of reports received from sources indicated in paragraph 3.4.6 above.

3.4.10 These investigations should be directed towards the gathering of sufficient evidence to establish whether the ship has violated the discharge requirements. Guidelines for the optimal collation of evidence are given in appendices 2 and 3.

3.4.11 If the investigations provide evidence that a violation of the discharge requirements took place within the jurisdiction of the port State, that port State should either cause proceedings to be taken in accordance with its law, or furnish to the flag State all information and evidence in its possession about the alleged violation. When the port State causes proceedings to be taken, it should inform the flag State.

3.4.12 Details of the report to be submitted to the flag State are set out in appendix 8.

3.4.13 The investigation might provide evidence that pollution was caused through damage to the ship or its equipment. This might indicate that a ship is not guilty of a violation of the discharge requirements of Annex I or II of MARPOL 73/78 provided that:

.1 all reasonable precautions have been taken after the occurrence of the damage or discovery of the discharge for the purpose of preventing or minimizing the discharge; and

.2 the owner or the master did not act either with intent to cause damage or recklessly and with knowledge that damage would probably result.

However, action by the port State as set out in chapter 4 may be called for.

Inspection of crude oil washing (COW) operations

3.4.14 Regulations 13 and 13B of Annex I of MARPOL 73/78, *inter alia*, require that crude oil washing of cargo tanks be performed on certain categories of crude carriers. A sufficient number of tanks shall be washed in order that ballast water is put only in cargo tanks which have been crude oil washed. The remaining cargo tanks shall be washed on a rotational basis for sludge control.

3.4.15 Port State authorities may carry out inspections to ensure that crude oil washing is performed by all crude carriers either required to have a COW system or where the owner or operator chooses to install a COW system in order to comply with regulation 13 of Annex I of MARPOL 73/78. In addition, compliance should be ensured with the operational requirements set out in the revised Specifications for the design, operation and control of crude oil washing systems (resolution A.446(XI)). This can best be done in the ports where the cargo is unloaded.

3.4.16 Parties should be aware that the inspection referred to in paragraph 3.4.15 may also lead to the identification of a pollution risk, necessitating additional action by the port State as set out in chapter 4.

3.4.17 Detailed guidelines for in-port inspections of crude oil washing procedures have been approved and published by IMO (*Crude Oil Washing Systems*, revised edition, 1983) and are set out in part 4 of appendix 2.

Inspection of unloading, stripping and prewash operations

3.4.18 Regulation 8 of Annex II of MARPOL 73/78 requires Parties to MARPOL 73/78 to appoint or authorize surveyors for the purpose of implementing the regulation.

3.4.19 The provisions of regulation 8 are aimed at ensuring in principle that a ship, having unloaded, to the maximum possible extent, noxious liquid substances of category A, B or C, proceeds to sea only if residues of such substances have been reduced to such quantities as may be discharged into the sea.

3.4.20 Compliance with these provisions is in principle ensured in the case of categories A, B and C substances through the application of a prewash in the unloading port and the discharge of prewash residue/water mixtures to reception facilities, except that in the case of non-solidifying and low-viscosity categories B and C substances, requirements for the efficient stripping of a tank to negligible quantities apply in lieu of the application of a prewash. Alternatively, for a number of substances, ventilation procedures may be employed for removing cargo residues from a tank.

3.4.21 Regulation 8 permits the Government of the receiving Party to exempt a ship proceeding to a port or terminal under the jurisdiction of another Party from the requirement to prewash cargo tanks and discharge residue/water mixtures to a reception facility provided:

.1   the ship does not wash or ballast cargo tanks prior to the next loading;

.2   the ship will prewash cargo tanks and discharge residue/water mixtures to a reception facility in another port; or

.3   the ship removes the cargo residues by ventilation.

3.4.22 Existing chemical tankers engaged on restricted voyages may by virtue of regulation 5A(6)(b) of Annex II of MARPOL 73/78 be exempted from the quantity limitation requirements entirely. If a cargo tank is to be ballasted or washed, a prewash is required after unloading category B or C substances and prewash residue/water mixtures must be discharged to shore reception facilities. The exemption should be indicated on the certificate.

3.4.23 A ship whose constructional and operational features are such that ballasting of cargo tanks is not required and cargo tank washing is only required for repairs or drydocking may by virtue of regulation 5A(7) be exempted from the provisions of paragraphs (1), (2), (3) and (4) of regulation 5A of Annex II of MARPOL 73/78 provided that all conditions mentioned in regulation 5A(7) are complied with. Consequentially, the certificate of the ship should indicate that each cargo tank is only certified for the carriage of one named substance. It should also indicate the particulars of the exemption granted by the Administration in respect of pumping, piping and discharge arrangements.

3.4.24 Detailed instructions on efficient stripping and prewash procedures are included in a ship's Procedures and Arrangements Manual. The Manual also contains alternative procedures to be followed in case of equipment failure.

3.4.25 Parties should be aware that the inspection referred to in 3.4.3 and 3.4.4 above may lead to the identification of a pollution risk or of a contravention of the discharge provisions, necessitating port State action as set out in chapter 4.

3.4.26 For details in respect of inspections under this section, reference is made to appendix 3.

3.5 Guidelines for control of operational requirements

3.5.1 When, during a port State control inspection, the PSCO has clear grounds according to section 2.3, the following on-board operational procedures may be checked in accordance with this resolution. However, in exercising controls recommended in these guidelines, the PSCO should not include any operational tests or impose physical demands which, in the judgement of the master, could jeopardize the safety of the ship, crew, passengers, control officers or cargo.

3.5.2 When carrying out operational control, the PSCO should ensure, as far as possible, no interference with normal shipboard operations, such as loading and unloading of cargo and ballasting, which is carried out under the responsibility of the master, nor should the PSCO require demonstration of operational aspects which would unnecessarily delay the ship.

3.5.3 Having assessed the extent to which operational requirements are complied with, the PSCO then has to exercise professional judgement to determine whether the operational proficiency of the crew as a whole is of a sufficient level to allow the ship to sail without danger to the ship or persons on board, or presenting an unreasonable threat of harm to the marine environment.

Muster list

3.5.4 The PSCO may determine if the crew members are aware of their duties indicated in the muster list.

3.5.5 The PSCO may ensure that muster lists are exhibited in conspicuous places throughout the ship, including the navigational bridge, the engine-room and the crew accommodation spaces. When determining if the muster list is in accordance with the regulations, the PSCO may verify whether:

.1 the muster list shows the duties assigned to the different members of the crew;

.2 the muster list specifies which officers are assigned to ensure that life-saving and fire appliances are maintained in good condition and are ready for immediate use;

21

.3   the muster list specifies the substitutes for key persons who may become disabled, taking into account that different emergencies may call for different actions;

.4   the muster list shows the duties assigned to crew members in relation to passengers in case of emergency;

.5   the format of the muster list used on passenger ships is approved.

3.5.6 To determine whether the muster list is up to date, the PSCO may require an up-to-date crew list, if available. Other possible means, e.g. Safe Manning Document, may be used for this purpose.

3.5.7 The PSCO may determine whether the duties assigned to crew members manning the survival craft (lifeboats or liferafts) are in accordance with the regulations and verify that a deck officer or certificated person is placed in charge of each survival craft to be used. However, the Administration (of the flag State), having due regard to the nature of the voyage, the number of persons on board and the characteristics of the ship, may permit persons practiced in the handling and operation of liferafts to be placed in charge of liferafts in lieu of persons qualified as above. A second-in-command should also be nominated in the case of lifeboats.

3.5.8 The PSCO may determine whether the crew members are familiar with the duties assigned to them in the muster list and are aware of the locations where they should perform their duties.

Communication

3.5.9 The PSCO may determine if the key crew members are able to communicate with each other, and with passengers as appropriate, in such a way that the safe operation of the ship is not impaired, especially in emergency situations.

3.5.10 The PSCO may ask the master which languages are used as the working languages.

3.5.11 The PSCO may ensure that the key crew members are able to understand each other during the inspection or drills. The crew members assigned to assist passengers should be able to give the necessary information to the passengers in case of an emergency.

Fire and abandon ship drills

3.5.12 The PSCO witnessing a fire and abandon ship drill should ensure that the crew members are familiar with their duties and the proper use of the ship's installations and equipment.

Fire drills

3.5.13 The PSCO may witness a fire drill carried out by the crew assigned to these duties on the muster list. After consultation with the master of the vessel, one or more specific locations of the ship may be selected for a simulated fire. A crew member may be sent to the location(s) and activate a fire alarm system or use other means to give alarm.

3.5.14 At the location the PSCO can describe the fire indication to the crew member and observe how the report of fire is relayed to the bridge or damage control centre. At this point most ships will sound the crew alarm to summon the fire-fighting parties to their stations. The PSCO should observe the fire-fighting party arriving on the scene, breaking out their equipment and fighting the simulated fire. Team leaders should be giving orders as appropriate to their crews and passing the word back to the bridge or damage control centre on the conditions. The fire-fighting crews should be observed for proper donning and the use of their equipment. The PSCO should make sure that all the gear is complete. Merely mustering the crew with their gear is not acceptable. Crew response to personnel injuries can be checked by selecting a crew member as a simulated casualty. The PSCO should observe how the word is passed and the response of stretcher and medical teams. Handling a stretcher properly through narrow passageways, doors and stairways is difficult and takes practice.

3.5.15 The drill should, as far as practicable, be conducted as if there was an actual emergency.

3.5.16 Those crew members assigned to other duties related to a fire drill, such as the manning of the emergency generators, the CO_2 room, the sprinkler and emergency fire pumps, should also be involved in the drill. The PSCO may ask these crew members to explain their duties and if possible to demonstrate their familiarity.

3.5.17 On passenger ships, special attention should be paid to the duties of those crew members assigned to the closing of manually operated doors and fire dampers. These closing devices should be operated by the responsible persons in the areas of the simulated fire(s) during the drill. Crew members not assigned to the fire-fighting teams are generally assigned to locations throughout the passenger accommodations to assist in passenger evacuation. These crew members should be asked to explain their duties and the meaning of the various emergency signals and asked to point out the two means of escape from the area, and where the passengers are to report. Crew members assigned to assist passengers should be able to communicate at least enough information to direct a passenger to the proper muster and embarkation stations.

Abandon ship drills

3.5.18 After consultation with the master, the PSCO may require an abandon ship drill for one or more survival craft. The essence of this drill is that the survival craft are manned and operated by the crew members assigned to them on the muster list. If possible, the PSCO should include the rescue boat(s) in this drill. SOLAS 74, chapter III, gives specific requirements on abandon ship training and drills, of which the following principles are particularly relevant.

3.5.19 The drill should, as far as practicable, be conducted as if there was an actual emergency.

3.5.20 The abandon ship drill should include:

.1 summoning of (passengers and) crew to the muster station(s) with the required alarm and ensuring that they are aware of the order to abandon ship as specified in the muster list;

.2 reporting to the stations and preparing for the duties described in the muster list;

.3 checking that (passengers and) crew are suitably dressed;

.4 checking that lifejackets are correctly donned;

.5 lowering of at least one lifeboat after the necessary preparation for launching;

.6 starting and operating the lifeboat engine; and

.7 operation of the davits used for launching liferafts.

3.5.21 If the lifeboat lowered during the drill is not the rescue boat, the rescue boat should be lowered as well, taking into account that it is boarded and launched in the shortest possible time. The PSCO should ensure that crew members are familiar with the duties assigned to them during abandon ship operations and that the crew member in charge of the survival craft has complete knowledge of the operation and equipment of the survival craft.

3.5.22 Each survival craft should be stowed in a state of continuous readiness so that two crew members can carry out preparations for embarking and launching in less than 5 minutes.

3.5.23 On passenger ships, it is required that lifeboats and davit-launched liferafts are capable of being launched within a period of 30 minutes.

3.5.24 On cargo ships, it is required that lifeboats and davit-launched liferafts are capable of being launched within a period of 10 minutes.

Damage control plan and Shipboard Oil Pollution Emergency Plan (SOPEP)

3.5.25 The PSCO may determine if a damage control plan is provided on a passenger ship and whether the crew members are familiar with their duties and the proper use of the ship's installations and equipment for damage control purposes. The same applies with regard to SOPEPs on all ships.

3.5.26 The PSCO may determine if the officers of the ship are aware of the contents of the damage control booklet which should be available to them, or of the damage control plan.

3.5.27 The officers may be asked to explain the action to be taken in various damage conditions.

3.5.28 The officers may also be asked to explain about the boundaries of the watertight compartments, the openings therein with the means of closure and position of any controls thereof and the arrangements for the correction of any list due to flooding.

3.5.29 The officers should have a sound knowledge of the effect of trim and stability of their ship in the event of damage to and consequent flooding of a compartment and counter-measures to be taken.

Fire control plan

3.5.30 The PSCO may determine if a fire control plan or booklet is provided and whether the crew members are familiar with the information given in the fire control plan or booklet.

3.5.31 The PSCO may verify that fire control plans are permanently exhibited for the guidance of the ship's officers. Alternatively, booklets containing the information of the fire control plan may be supplied to each officer, and one copy should at all times be available on board in an accessible position. Plans and booklets should be kept up to date, any alterations being recorded thereon as soon as possible.

3.5.32 The PSCO may determine that the responsible officers, especially those who are assigned to related duties on the muster list, are aware of the information provided by the fire control plan or booklet and how to act in case of a fire.

3.5.33 The PSCO may ensure that the officers in charge of the ship are familiar with the principal structural members which form part of the various fire sections and the means of access to the different compartments.

Bridge operation

3.5.34 The PSCO may determine if officers in charge of a navigational watch are familiar with bridge control and navigational equipment, changing the steering mode from automatic to manual and vice versa, and the ship's manoeuvring characteristics.

3.5.35 The officer in charge of a navigational watch should have knowledge of the location and operation of all safety and navigational equipment. Moreover, this officer should be familiar with procedures which apply to the navigation of the ship in all circumstances and should be aware of all information available.

3.5.36 The PSCO may also verify the familiarity of the officers with all the information available to them such as manoeuvring characteristics of the ship, life-saving signals, up-to-date nautical publications, checklists concerning bridge procedures, instructions, manuals, etc.

3.5.37 The PSCO may verify the familiarity of the officers with procedures such as periodical tests and checks of equipment, preparations for arrival and departure, change over of steering modes, signalling, communications, manoeuvring, emergencies and log-book entries.

Cargo operation

3.5.38 The PSCO may determine if ship's personnel assigned specific duties related to the cargo and cargo equipment are familiar with those duties, any dangers posed by the cargo and with the measures to be taken in such a context.

3.5.39 With respect to the carriage of solid bulk cargoes, the PSCO should verify, as appropriate, that cargo loading is performed in accordance with a ship's loading plan and unloading in accordance with a ship's unloading plan agreed by the ship and the terminal.

3.5.40 The PSCO, when appropriate, may determine whether the responsible crew members are familiar with the relevant provisions of the Code of Safe Practice for Solid Bulk Cargoes, particularly those concerning moisture limits and trimming of the cargo, the Code of Safe Practice for Ships Carrying Timber Deck Cargoes and the Code of Safe Practice for Cargo Stowage and Securing.

3.5.41 Some solid materials transported in bulk can present a hazard during transport because of their chemical nature or physical properties. Section 2 of the Code of Safe Practice for Solid Bulk Cargoes gives general precautions. Section 4 of the Code of Safe Practice for Solid Bulk Cargoes contains the obligation imposed on the shipper to provide all necessary information to ensure a safe transport of the cargo. The PSCO may determine whether all relevant details, including all relevant certificates of tests, have been provided to the master from the shipper.

3.5.42 For some cargoes, such as cargoes which are subject to liquefaction, special precautions are given (see section 7 of the BC Code). The PSCO may determine whether all precautions are met, with special attention for the stability of those vessels engaged in the transport of cargoes subject to liquefaction and solid hazardous waste in bulk.

3.5.43 Officers responsible for cargo handling and operation and key crew members of oil tankers, chemical tankers and liquefied gas carriers should be familiar with the cargo and cargo equipment and with the safety measures as stipulated in the relevant sections of the IBC and IGC Codes.

3.5.44 For the carriage of grain in bulk, reference is made to part C, chapter VI of SOLAS 74 and the International Code for the Safe Carriage of Grain in Bulk (resolution MSC.23(59)).

3.5.45 The PSCO may determine whether the operations and loading manuals include all the relevant information for safe loading and unloading operations in port as well as in transit conditions.

Operation of the machinery

3.5.46 The PSCO may determine if responsible ship's personnel are familiar with their duties related to operating essential machinery, such as:

    .1   emergency and stand-by sources of electrical power;

    .2   auxiliary steering gear;

    .3   bilge and fire pumps; and

    .4   any other equipment essential in emergency situations.

3.5.47 The PSCO may verify whether the responsible ship's personnel are familiar with, *inter alia*:

   .1   Emergency generator:

   .1.1   actions which are necessary before the engine can be started;

   .1.2   different possibilities to start the engine in combination with the source of starting energy; and

   .1.3   procedures when the first attempts to start the engine fail.

   .2   Stand-by generator engine:

   .2.1   possibilities to start the stand-by engine, automatic or by hand;

   .2.2   blackout procedures; and

   .2.3   load-sharing system.

3.5.48 The PSCO may verify whether the responsible ship's personnel are familiar with, *inter alia*:

   .1   which type of auxiliary steering gear system applies to the ship;

   .2   how it is indicated which steering gear unit is in operation; and

   .3   what action is needed to bring the auxiliary steering gear into operation.

3.5.49 The PSCO may verify whether the responsible ship's personnel are familiar with, *inter alia*:

   .1   Bilge pumps:

   .1.1   number and location of bilge pumps installed on board the ship (including emergency bilge pumps);

   .1.2   starting procedures for all these bilge pumps;

   .1.3   appropriate valves to operate; and

   .1.4   most likely causes of failure of bilge pump operation and their possible remedies.

   .2   Fire pumps:

   .2.1   number and location of fire pumps installed on board the ship (including the emergency fire pump);

   .2.2   starting procedures for all these pumps; and

   .2.3   appropriate valves to operate.

3.5.50 The PSCO may verify whether the responsible ship's personnel are familiar with, *inter alia*:

.1   starting and maintenance of lifeboat engine and/or rescue boat engine;

.2   local control procedures for those systems which are normally controlled from the navigating bridge;

.3   use of the emergency and fully independent sources of electrical power of radio installations;

.4   maintenance procedures for batteries;

.5   emergency stops, fire detection system and alarm system operation of watertight and fire doors (stored energy systems); and

.6   change of control from automatic to manual for cooling water and lube oil systems for main and auxiliary engines.

Manuals, instructions, etc.

3.5.51 The PSCO may determine if the appropriate crew members are able to understand the information given in manuals, instructions, etc., relevant to the safe condition and operation of the ship and its equipment and that they are aware of the requirements for maintenance, periodical testing, training, drills and recording of log-book entries.

3.5.52 The following information should, *inter alia,* be provided on board and PSCOs may determine whether it is in a language or languages understood by the crew and whether crew members concerned are aware of the contents and are able to respond accordingly:

.1   instructions concerning the maintenance and operation of all the equipment and installations on board for the fighting and containment of fire should be kept under one cover, readily available in an accessible position;

.2   clear instructions to be followed in the event of an emergency should be provided for every person on board;

.3   illustrations and instructions in appropriate languages should be posted in passenger cabins and be conspicuously displayed at muster stations and other passenger spaces to inform passengers of their muster station, the essential action they must take in an emergency and the method of donning lifejackets;

.4   posters and signs should be provided on or in the vicinity of survival craft and their launching controls and shall illustrate the purpose of controls and the procedures for operating the appliance and give relevant instructions or warnings;

.5　instructions for on-board maintenance of life-saving appliances;

.6　training manuals should be provided in each crew mess-room and recreation room or in each crew cabin. The training manual, which may comprise several volumes, should contain instructions and information, in easily understood terms illustrated wherever possible, on the life-saving appliances provided in the ship and on the best method of survival;

.7　Shipboard Oil Pollution Emergency Plan in accordance with MARPOL 73/78, Annex I, regulation 26; and

.8　stability booklet, associated stability plans and stability information.

Oil and oily mixtures from machinery spaces

3.5.53　The PSCO may determine if all operational requirements of Annex I of MARPOL 73/78 have been met, taking into account:

.1　the quantity of oil residues generated;

.2　the capacity of sludge and bilge water holding tank; and

.3　the capacity of the oily-water separator.

3.5.54　An inspection of the Oil Record Book should be made. The PSCO may determine if reception facilities have been used and note any alleged inadequacy of such facilities.

3.5.55　The PSCO may determine whether the responsible officer is familiar with the handling of sludge and bilge water. The relevant items from the guidelines for systems for handling oily wastes in machinery spaces of ships may be used as guidance. Taking into account the above, the PSCO may determine if the ullage of the sludge tank is sufficient for the expected generated sludge during the next intended voyage. The PSCO may verify that, in respect of ships for which the Administration has waived the requirements of regulation 16(1) and (2) to Annex I of MARPOL 73/78, all oily bilge water is retained on board for subsequent discharge to a reception facility.

3.5.56　When reception facilities in other ports have not been used because of inadequacy, the PSCO should advise the master to report the inadequacy of the reception facility to the ship's flag State, in conformity with MEPC/Circ.349 of 18 November 1998.

Loading, unloading and cleaning procedures for cargo spaces of tankers

3.5.57 The PSCO may determine if all operational requirements of Annexes I or II of MARPOL 73/78 have been met, taking into account the type of tanker and the type of cargo carried, including the inspection of the Oil Record Book and/or Cargo Record Book. The PSCO may determine if the reception facilities have been used and note any alleged inadequacy of such facilities.

3.5.58 For the control on loading, unloading and cleaning procedures for tankers carrying oil, reference is made to paragraphs 3.4.14 to 3.4.17 above, where guidance is given for the inspection of crude oil washing (COW) operations. Appendix 2, part 4, gives detailed guidelines for in-port inspection of crude oil washing procedures.

3.5.59 For the control on loading, unloading and cleaning procedures for tankers carrying noxious liquid substances, reference is made to paragraphs 3.4.18 to 3.4.26 above, where guidance is given for the inspection of unloading, stripping and prewash operations. More detailed guidelines for these inspections are given in appendix 3, part 4.

3.5.60 When reception facilities in other ports have not been used because of inadequacy, the PSCO should advise the master to report the inadequacy of the reception facility to the ship's flag State, in conformity with MEPC/Circ.349 of 18 November 1998.

3.5.61 When a vessel is permitted to proceed to the next port with residues of noxious liquid substances on board in excess of those permitted to be discharged into the sea during the ship's passage, it should be ascertained that the residues can be received by that port. At the same time that port should be informed, if practicable.

Dangerous goods and harmful substances in packaged form

3.5.62 The PSCO may determine if the required shipping documents for the carriage of dangerous goods and harmful substances carried in packaged form are provided on board and whether the dangerous goods and harmful substances are properly stowed and segregated and the crew members are familiar with the essential action to be taken in an emergency involving such packaged cargo.

3.5.63 Ship types and cargo spaces of ships built after 1 September 1984 intended for the carriage of dangerous goods should comply with the requirements of SOLAS regulation II-2/54, in addition to the requirements of regulation II-2/53 (for cargo ships) and the requirements of regulations II-2/3 and II-2/39 (for passenger ships), unless such requirements have already been met by compliance with requirements elsewhere in the Convention. The only exemption permissible is when dangerous goods in limited quantities are carried.

3.5.64 Annex III of MARPOL 73/78 contains requirements for the carriage of harmful substances in packaged form which are identified in the IMDG Code as marine pollutants. Cargoes which are determined to be marine pollutants should be labelled and stowed in accordance with Annex III of MARPOL 73/78.

3.5.65 The PSCO may determine whether a Document of Compliance is on board and whether the ship's personnel are familiar with this document provided by the Administration as evidence of compliance of construction and equipment with the requirements. Additional control may consist of:

.1   ascertaining whether the dangerous goods have been stowed on board in conformity with the Document of Compliance, using the dangerous goods manifest or the stowage plan, required by SOLAS chapter VII. This manifest or stowage plan may be combined with the one required under Annex III of MARPOL 73/78;

.2   ascertaining whether inadvertent pumping of leaking flammable or toxic liquids is not possible in case these substances are carried in under-deck cargo spaces; and

.3   determining whether the ship's personnel are familiar with the relevant provisions of the Medical First Aid Guide and Emergency Procedures for Ships Carrying Dangerous Goods.

Garbage

3.5.66 The PSCO may determine if all operational requirements of Annex V of MARPOL 73/78 have been met. The PSCO may determine if the reception facilities have been used and note any alleged inadequacy of such facilities.

3.5.67 "Guidelines for the implementation of Annex V of MARPOL 73/78" were approved by the MEPC at its twenty-ninth session and have been published. One of the objectives of these guidelines is "to assist vessel operators complying with the requirements set forth in Annex V and domestic laws".

3.5.68 The PSCO may determine whether:

.1   ship's personnel are aware of these Guidelines, in particular section 3 "Minimizing the amount of potential garbage" and section 4 "Shipboard garbage handling and storage procedures"; and

.2   ship's personnel are familiar with the disposal and discharge requirements under Annex V of MARPOL 73/78 inside and outside a Special Area and are aware of the areas determined as Special Areas under Annex V of MARPOL 73/78.

3.5.69 When reception facilities in other ports have not been used because of inadequacy, the PSCO should advise the master to report the inadequacy of the reception facility to the ship's flag State, in conformity with MEPC/Circ.349 of 18 November 1998.

3.6   Minimum manning standards and certification

Introduction

3.6.1 The guiding principles for port State control of the manning of a foreign ship should be to establish conformity with:

.1   the flag State's safe manning requirements. Where this is in doubt, the flag State should be consulted; and

.2   the international provisions as laid down in SOLAS 74, STCW 78 and resolution A.481(XII).

Manning control

3.6.2 If a ship is manned in accordance with a Safe Manning Document or equivalent document issued by the flag State, the PSCO should accept that the ship is safely manned unless the document has clearly been issued without regard to the principles contained in the relevant instruments, in which case the PSCO should act according to the procedures defined in paragraph 3.6.4 below.

3.6.3 If the actual crew number or composition does not conform with the manning document, the port State should ask the flag State for advice whether the ship should be allowed to sail with the actual number of crew and its composition. Such a request and response should be by expedient means and either Party may request this communication in writing. If the actual crew number or composition is not brought into accordance with the safe manning document or the flag State does not advise that the ship can sail, the ship may be considered for detention, after the criteria set out in paragraph 3.6.8 below have been taken into proper account.

3.6.4 If the ship does not carry a safe manning document or equivalent, the port State should request the flag State to specify the required number of crew and its composition and to issue a relevant document as quickly as possible.

3.6.5 In case the actual number or composition of the crew does not conform with the specifications received from the flag State, the procedure contained in paragraph 3.6.3 applies.

3.6.6 If the flag State does not respond to the request, this should be considered as clear grounds for a more detailed inspection to ensure that the number and composition of the crew is in accordance with the principles laid down in paragraph 3.6.1. The ship should only be allowed to proceed to sea if it is safe to do so, taking into account the criteria for detention indicated in paragraph 3.6.8. In any such case the minimum standards to be applied should be no more stringent than those applied to ships flying the flag of the port State.

Control under the provisions of STCW 78

3.6.7 Control exercised by the PSCO should be limited to the following:

.1   verification that all seafarers serving on board, who are required to be certificated, hold an appropriate certificate or a valid dispensation, or provide documentary proof that an application for an endorsement has been submitted to the Administration;

.2   verification that the numbers and certificates of the seafarers serving on board are in conformity with the applicable safe manning requirements of the Administration; and

.3   assessment of the ability of the seafarers of the ship to maintain watchkeeping standards as required by the Convention if there are clear grounds for believing that such standards are not being maintained because any of the following have occurred:

.3.1   the ship has been involved in a collision, grounding or stranding, or

.3.2   there has been a discharge of substances from the ship when under way, at anchor or at berth, which is illegal under any international convention, or

.3.3   the ship has been manoeuvred in an erratic or unsafe manner whereby routeing measures adopted by the Organization or safe navigation practices and procedures have not been followed, or

.3.4   the ship is otherwise being operated in such a manner as to pose a danger to persons, property or the environment.[*]

---

[*] Applicable from 1 February 1997.

Detention related to minimum manning standards and certificatio

3.6.8 Before detaining a ship, the following should be consider

   .1   length and nature of the intended voyage or service;

   .2   whether the deficiency poses a danger to ships, persons on board or the environment;

   .3   whether appropriate rest periods of the crew can be observed;

   .4   size and type of ship and equipment provided; and

   .5   nature of cargo.

3.7   Guidelines for port State control related to the ISM Code

3.7.1 To the extent applicable, the PSCO should examine the copy of the Document of Compliance (DOC), issued to the company, and the Safety Management Certificate (SMC), issued to the ship. An SMC is not valid unless the company holds a valid DOC for that ship type. The PSCO should in particular verify that the type of ship is included in the DOC and that the company's particulars are the same on both the DOC and the SMC.

3.7.2 During the examination of on-board documents and certificates, PSCOs should recognize:

   .1   that differences may exist between the classification societies' designation of *"bulk carrier"* that appear on the class certificate as defined in their individual Rules, versus the interpretation of *"bulk carrier"* contained in SOLAS/CONF.4/25, annex, resolution 6 and that the latter definition should be used to determine if the ship should have been certified by 1 July 1998;

   .2   the common practice of issuing, after successfully completing an audit, SMCs and DOCs valid for a period not exceeding 5 months, to cover the period between completion of the audit and issuance of the full-term certificate by either the Administration or the recognized organization; and

   .3   that the current valid DOC with proper annual endorsements is normally only available in the company to which it has been issued and that the copy on board may not reflect the annual endorsements that exist on the valid DOC held by the company.

3.7.3 If a vessel has been issued with Interim Certificates (DOC and/or SMC), the PSCO should check whether they have been issued in accordance with the provisions of paragraphs 3.3.2 and 3.3.4 of resolution A.788(19).

3.7.4 A more detailed inspection of the Safety Management System (SMS) should be carried out if clear grounds are established. Clear grounds may include absent or inaccurate ISM Code certification or detainable or many non-detainable deficiencies in other areas.

3.7.5 When carrying out a more detailed inspection, the PSCO may utilize, but not be limited to, the following questions to ascertain the extent of compliance with the ISM Code (references to the relevant paragraphs of the ISM Code are given in *italic* print in brackets).

.1 Is there a company safety and environmental protection policy and is the appropriate ship's personnel familiar with it? (*2.2*)

.2 Is safety management documentation (e.g. manual) readily available on board? (*11.3*)

.3 Is relevant documentation on the SMS in a working language or language understood by the ship's personnel? (*6.6*)

.4 Can senior ship officers identify the company responsible for the operation of the ship and does this correspond with the entity specified on the ISM Code certificates? (*3*)

.5 Can senior ship officers identify the "designated person"? (*4*)

.6 Are procedures in place for establishing and maintaining contact with shore management in an emergency? (*8.3*)

.7 Are programmes for drills and exercises to prepare for emergency actions available on board? (*8.2*)

.8 How have new crew members been made familiar with their duties if they have recently joined the ship and are instructions which are essential prior to sailing available? (*6.3*)

.9 Can the master provide documented proof of his responsibilities and authority, which must include his overriding authority? (*5*)

.10 Have non-conformities been reported to the company and has corrective action been taken by the company? PSCOs should not normally scrutinise the contents of any Non Conformity Note (NCN) resulting from internal audits. (*9.1, 9.2*)

.11 Does the ship have a maintenance routine and are records available? (*10.2*)

3.7.6 Deficiencies in the Safety Management System should be recorded in the PSCO's inspection report. The port State authority should, if necessary, inform the flag State of deficiencies found in the SMS. Those deficiencies identified in the SMS which are defined as major non-conformities in resolution A.788(19) have to be rectified before sailing. The procedures set out in chapter 4 are applicable.

Chapter 4
Contravention and detention

4.1   Identification of a substandard ship

4.1.1 In general, a ship is regarded as substandard if the hull, machinery, equipment, or operational safety is substantially below the standards required by the relevant conventions or if its crew is not in conformance with the safe manning document, owing to, *inter alia:*

.1   the absence of principal equipment or arrangements required by the conventions;

.2   non-compliance of equipment or arrangements with relevant specifications of the conventions;

.3   substantial deterioration of the ship or its equipment, for example, because of poor maintenance;

.4   insufficient operational proficiency, or unfamiliarity of the crew with essential operational procedures; and

.5   insufficiency of manning or insufficiency of certification of seafarers.

4.1.2 If these evident factors as a whole or individually make the ship unseaworthy and put at risk the ship or the life of persons on board or present an unreasonable threat of harm to the marine environment if it were allowed to proceed to sea, it should be regarded as a substandard ship.

4.2   Submission of information concerning deficiencies

4.2.1 Information that a ship appears to be substandard should be submitted to the appropriate authorities of the port State (see section 4.3 below) by a member of the crew, a professional body, an association, a trade union or any other individual with an interest in the safety of the ship, its crew and passengers, or the protection of the marine environment.

4.2.2 This information should be submitted in writing to permit proper documentation of the case and of the alleged deficiencies. When the information is passed verbally, the filing of a written report should be required, identifying, for the purposes of the port State's records, the individual or body providing the information. The attending PSCO may collect this information and submit it as part of the PSCO's report if the originator is unable to do so.

4.2.3 Information which may cause an investigation should be submitted as early as possible after the arrival of the ship, thereby giving adequate time to the authorities to act as necessary.

4.2.4 Each Party to the relevant convention should determine which authorities should receive information on substandard ships and initiate action. Measures should be taken to ensure that information submitted to the wrong department is promptly passed on by such department to the appropriate authority for action.

4.3   Port State action in response to alleged substandard ships

4.3.1 On receipt of information about an alleged substandard ship or alleged pollution risk, the authorities should immediately investigate the matter and take action required by the circumstances in accordance with the preceding sections.

4.3.2 Authorities receiving information about a substandard ship which could give rise to detention should forthwith notify any maritime, consular and/or diplomatic representatives of the flag State in the area of the ship and request them to initiate or co-operate with investigations. Likewise, the recognized organization which has issued the relevant certificates on behalf of the flag State should be notified. However, these provisions will not relieve the authorities of the port State, being a Party to a relevant convention, of the responsibility for taking appropriate action in accordance with its powers under the relevant conventions.

4.3.3 If the port State receiving information is unable to take action because there is insufficient time or no PSCOs can be made available before the ship sails, the information should be passed to the authorities of the country of the next appropriate port of call, to the flag State and also to the recognized organization in that port, where appropriate.

4.4   Responsibilities of port State to take remedial action

When a PSCO determines that a ship can be regarded as substandard, as specified in section 4.1 and appendix 1, the port State should immediately ensure that corrective action is taken to safeguard the safety of the ship and its passengers and/or crew and eliminate any threat of harm to the marine environment before permitting the ship to sail.

4.5   Guidance for the detention of ships

Notwithstanding the fact that it is impracticable to define a ship as substandard solely by reference to a list of qualifying defects, guidance for the detention of ships is given in appendix 1.

4.6 Suspension of inspection

4.6.1 In exceptional circumstances where, as a result of a more detailed inspection, the overall condition of a ship and its equipment, also taking into account the crew conditions, are found to be obviously substandard, the PSCO may suspend an inspection.

4.6.2 Prior to suspending an inspection, the PSCO should have recorded detainable deficiencies in the areas set out in appendix 1, as appropriate.

4.6.3 The suspension of the inspection may continue until the responsible parties have taken the steps necessary to ensure that the ship complies with the requirements of the relevant instruments.

4.6.4 In cases where the ship is detained and an inspection is suspended, the port State authority should notify the responsible parties without delay. The notification should include information about the detention and state that the inspection is suspended until the port State authority has been informed that the ship complies with all relevant requirements.

4.7 Procedures for rectification of deficiencies and release

4.7.1 The PSCO should endeavour to ensure the rectification of all deficiencies detected.

4.7.2 In the case of deficiencies which are clearly hazardous to safety or the environment, the PSCO should, except as provided in paragraph 4.7.3, ensure that the hazard is removed before the ship is allowed to proceed to sea. For this purpose, appropriate action should be taken, which may include detention or a formal prohibition of a ship to continue an operation due to established deficiencies which, individually or together, would render the continued operation hazardous.

4.7.3 Where deficiencies which caused a detention as referred to in paragraph 4.7.2 cannot be remedied in the port of inspection, the port State authority may allow the ship concerned to proceed to the nearest appropriate repair yard available, as chosen by the master and agreed to by that authority, provided that the conditions agreed between the port State authority and the flag State are complied with. Such conditions will ensure that the ship should not sail until it can proceed without risk to the safety of the passengers or crew, or risk to other ships, or without being an unreasonable threat of harm to the marine environment. Such conditions may include confirmation from the flag States that remedial action has been taken on the ship in question. In such circumstances the port State authority will notify the authority of the ship's next port of call, the parties mentioned in paragraph 5.1.4 and any other authority, as appropriate.

Notification to authorities should be made in the form shown in appendix 6. The authority receiving such notification should inform the notifying authority of action taken and may use the form shown in appendix 7.

4.7.4 On the condition that all possible efforts have been made to rectify all other deficiencies, except those referred to in paragraphs 4.7.2 and 4.7.3, the ship may be allowed to proceed to a port where any such deficiencies can be rectified.

4.7.5 If a ship referred to in paragraph 4.7.3 proceeds to sea without complying with the conditions agreed to by the authority of the port of inspection, that port State authority should immediately alert the next port, if known, the flag State and all other authorities it considers appropriate.

4.7.6 If a ship referred to in paragraph 4.7.3 does not call at the nominated repair port, the port State authority of the repair port should immediately alert the flag State and detaining port State, which may take appropriate action, and notify any other authority it considers appropriate.

Chapter 5
Reporting requirements

5.1 Port State reporting

5.1.1 Port State authorities should ensure that, on the conclusion of an inspection, the master of the ship is provided with a document giving the results of the inspection, details of any action taken by the PSCO, and a list of any corrective action to be initiated by the master and/or company. Such reports should be made in accordance with the format in appendix 5.

5.1.2 Where, in the exercise of port State control, a Party denies a foreign ship entry to the ports or offshore terminals under its jurisdiction, whether or not as a result of information about a substandard ship, it should forthwith provide the master and flag State with reasons for the denial of entry.

5.1.3 In the case of a detention, notification should be made to the flag State administration. If such notification is made verbally, it should be subsequently confirmed in writing. Likewise, the recognized organizations which have issued the relevant certificates on behalf of the flag State should be notified, where appropriate.

5.1.4 If the ship has been allowed to sail with known deficiencies, the authorities of the port State should communicate all the facts to the authorities of the country of the next appropriate port of call, to the flag State, and to the recognized organization, where appropriate.

5.1.5 Parties to a relevant convention, when they have exercised control giving rise to detention, should submit to the Organization reports in accordance with regulation 19 of chapter I of SOLAS 74, article 11 of MARPOL 73/78, article 21 of Load Lines 66, or article X(3) of STCW 78. Such deficiency reports should be made in accordance with the form given in appendix 5 or 8, as appropriate.

5.1.6 Copies of such deficiency reports should, in addition to being forwarded to the Organization, be sent by the port State without delay to the authorities of the flag State and, where appropriate, to the recognized organization which had issued the relevant certificate. Deficiencies found which are not related to the applicable conventions, or which involve ships of non-convention countries or below convention size, should be submitted to flag States and/or to appropriate organizations but not to IMO.

5.1.7 Relevant telephone numbers and addresses of flag State headquarters to which reports should be sent as outlined above as well as addresses of flag State offices which provide inspection services should be provided to the Organization.*

5.2 Flag State reporting

5.2.1 On receiving a report on detention, the flag State and, where appropriate, the recognized organization through the flag State administration should, as soon as possible, inform the Organization of remedial action taken in respect of the detention. A format in which this information should be transmitted is shown in appendix 9.

5.2.2 Relevant telephone numbers and addresses of port State control offices, headquarters and those who provide inspection services should be provided to the Organization.

5.3 Reporting of allegations under MARPOL 73/78

5.3.1 A report on alleged deficiencies or on alleged contravention of the discharge provisions relating to the provisions of MARPOL 73/78 should be forwarded to the flag State as soon as possible, preferably no later than sixty days after the observation of the deficiencies or contravention. Such reports may be made in accordance with the format in appendix 5 or 8, as appropriate. If a contravention of the discharge provisions is suspected, then the information should be supplemented by evidence of violations which, as a minimum, should include the information specified in parts 2 and 3 of appendices 2 and 3 of these Procedures.

5.3.2 On receiving a report on alleged deficiencies or alleged contravention of the discharge provisions, the flag State and, where appropriate, the recognized organization through the flag State administration, should, as soon as possible, inform the Party submitting the report of its immediate action taken in respect of the alleged deficiencies or contravention. That Party and IMO should, upon completion of such action, be informed of the outcome and details, where appropriate, be included in the mandatory annual report to IMO.

---

* Such addresses are available in MSC/Circ.971–MEPC.6/Circ.6, and the IMO Internet Home Page (www.imo.org).

Chapter 6
Review procedures

6.1 Report of comments

6.1.1 In the interest of making information regarding deficiencies and remedial measures generally available, a summary of such reports should be made by the Organization in a timely manner in order that the information can be disseminated in accordance with the Organization's procedures to all Parties to the applicable conventions. In the summary of deficiency reports, an indication should be given of flag State action or whether a comment by the flag State concerned is outstanding.

6.1.2 The appropriate IMO Committee should periodically evaluate the summary of the deficiency reports in order to identify measures that may be necessary to ensure more consistent and effective application of IMO instruments, paying close attention to the difficulties reported by Parties to the relevant conventions, particularly in respect to developing countries in their capacity as port States.

6.1.3 Recommendations to rectify such difficulties when recognized by the appropriate IMO Committee, should, where appropriate, be incorporated into the applicable IMO instrument and any modifications relating to the procedures and obligations should be made in the port State documentation.

Appendix 1
Guidelines for the detention of ships

1   Introduction

1.1   When deciding whether the deficiencies found in a ship are sufficiently serious to merit detention the PSCO should assess whether:

    .1   the ship has relevant, valid documentation;

    .2   the ship has the crew required in the Minimum Safe Manning Document.

1.2   During inspection, the PSCO should further assess whether the ship and/or crew, throughout its forthcoming voyage, is able to:

    .1   navigate safely;

    .2   safely handle, carry and monitor the condition of the cargo;

    .3   operate the engine-room safely;

    .4   maintain proper propulsion and steering;

    .5   fight fires effectively in any part of the ship if necessary;

    .6   abandon ship speedily and safely and effect rescue if necessary;

    .7   prevent pollution of the environment;

    .8   maintain adequate stability;

    .9   maintain adequate watertight integrity;

    .10   communicate in distress situations if necessary; and

    .11   provide safe and healthy conditions on board.

1.3   If the result of any of these assessments is negative, taking into account all deficiencies found, the ship should be strongly considered for detention. A combination of deficiencies of a less serious nature may also warrant the detention of the ship. Ships which are unsafe to proceed to sea should be detained upon the first inspection irrespective of the time the ship will stay in port.

2   General

The lack of valid certificates as required by the relevant instruments may warrant the detention of ships. However, ships flying the flag of States not a Party to a convention or not having implemented another relevant instrument are not entitled to carry the certificates provided for by the convention or other relevant instrument. Therefore, absence of the required certificates should not by itself constitute a reason to detain these ships; however, in applying the no more favourable treatment clause, substantial compliance with the provisions and criteria specified in this document must be required before the ship sails.

3   Detainable deficiencies

To assist the PSCO in the use of these guidelines, there follows a list of deficiencies, grouped under relevant conventions and/or codes, which are considered to be of such a serious nature that they may warrant the detention of the ship involved. This list is not considered exhaustive but is intended to give examples of relevant items.

Areas under the SOLAS Convention

1   Failure of proper operation of propulsion and other essential machinery, as well as electrical installations.

2   Insufficient cleanliness of engine-room, excess amount of oily-water mixture in bilges, insulation of piping including exhaust pipes in engine-room contaminated by oil, and improper operation of bilge pumping arrangements.

3   Failure of proper operation of emergency generator, lighting, batteries and switches.

4   Failure of proper operation of the main and auxiliary steering gear.

5   Absence, insufficient capacity or serious deterioration of personal life-saving appliances, survival craft and launching arrangements.

6   Absence, non-compliance or substantial deterioration, to the extent that it cannot comply with its intended use, of fire detection system, fire alarms, fire-fighting equipment, fixed fire-extinguishing installation, ventilation valves, fire dampers and quick-closing devices.

7   Absence, substantial deterioration or failure of proper operation of the cargo deck area fire protection on tankers.

8   Absence, non-compliance or serious deterioration of lights, shapes or sound signals.

9   Absence or failure of proper operation of the radio equipment for distress and safety communication.

10   Absence or failure of proper operation of navigation equipment, taking into account the relevant provisions of SOLAS regulation V/12(o).

11 Absence of corrected navigational charts and/or all other relevant nautical publications necessary for the intended voyage, taking into account that electronic charts may be used as a substitute for the charts.

12 Absence of non-sparking exhaust ventilation for cargo pump-rooms.

13 Serious deficiency in the operational requirements listed in paragraphs 3.5.1 to 3.5.69.

14 Number, composition or certification of crew not corresponding with safe manning document.

15 Non-implementation of the enhanced programme of inspection under resolution A.744(18).

Areas under the IBC Code

1 Transport of a substance not mentioned in the Certificate of Fitness or missing cargo information.

2 Missing or damaged high-pressure safety devices.

3 Electrical installations not intrinsically safe or not corresponding to the Code requirements.

4 Sources of ignition in hazardous locations.

5 Contravention of special requirements.

6 Exceeding of maximum allowable cargo quantity per tank.

7 Insufficient heat protection for sensitive products.

Areas under the IGC Code

1 Transport of a substance not mentioned in the Certificate of Fitness or missing cargo information.

2 Missing closing devices for accommodation or service spaces.

3 Bulkhead not gastight.

4 Defective air locks.

5 Missing or defective quick-closing valves.

6 Missing or defective safety valves.

7 Electrical installations not intrinsically safe or not corresponding to the Code requirements.

8 Ventilators in cargo area not operable.

9   Pressure alarms for cargo tanks not operable.

10   Gas detection plant and/or toxic gas detection plant defective.

11   Transport of substances to be inhibited without a valid inhibitor certificate.

Areas under the Load Lines Convention

1   Significant areas of damage or corrosion, or pitting of plating and associated stiffening in decks and hull affecting seaworthiness or strength to take local loads, unless properly authorized temporary repairs for a voyage to a port for permanent repairs have been carried out.

2   A recognized case of insufficient stability.

3   The absence of sufficient and reliable information, in an approved form, which by rapid and simple means enables the master to arrange for the loading and ballasting of the ship in such a way that a safe margin of stability is maintained at all stages and at varying conditions of the voyage, and that the creation of any unacceptable stresses in the ship's structure is avoided.

4   Absence, substantial deterioration or defective closing devices, hatch closing arrangements and watertight/weathertight doors.

5   Overloading.

6   Absence of, or impossibility to read, draught marks and/or load line marks.

Areas under the MARPOL Convention, Annex I

1   Absence, serious deterioration or failure of proper operation of the oily-water filtering equipment, the oil discharge monitoring and control system or the 15 ppm alarm arrangements.

2   Remaining capacity of slop and/or sludge tank insufficient for the intended voyage.

3   Oil Record Book not available.

4   Unauthorized discharge bypass fitted.

5   Failure to meet the requirements of regulation 13G(4) or alternative requirements specified in regulation 13G(7).

Areas under the MARPOL Convention, Annex II

1   Absence of P and A Manual.

2   Cargo is not categorized.

3   No Cargo Record Book available.

4   Transport of oil-like substances without satisfying the requirements.

5   Unauthorized discharge bypass fitted.

Areas under the STCW Convention

1   Failure of seafarers to hold a certificate, to have an appropriate certificate, to have a valid dispensation or to provide documentary proof that an application for an endorsement has been submitted to the Administration.

2   Failure to comply with the applicable safe manning requirements of the Administration.

3   Failure of navigational or engineering watch arrangements to conform with the requirements specified for the ship by the Administration.

4   Absence in a watch of a person qualified to operate equipment essential for safe navigation, safety radiocommunications or the prevention of marine pollution.

5   Inability to provide for the first watch at the commencement of a voyage and for subsequent relieving watches persons who are sufficiently rested and otherwise fit for duty.

Areas which may not warrant a detention, but where, e.g., cargo operations have to be suspended

Failure of proper operation (or maintenance) of inert gas system, cargo-related gear or machinery will be considered sufficient grounds to stop cargo operation.

Appendix 2

Guidelines for investigations and inspections carried out under Annex I of MARPOL 73/78

Part 1
Inspection of IOPP Certificate, ship and equipment

1   **Ships required to carry an IOPP Certificate**

1.1   On boarding and introduction to the master or responsible ship's officer, the PSCO should examine the IOPP Certificate, including the attached Record of Construction and Equipment, and the Oil Record Book.

1.2   The certificate carries information on the type of ship and the dates of surveys and inspections. As a preliminary check it should be confirmed that the dates of surveys and inspections are still valid. Furthermore it should be established if the ship carries an oil cargo and whether the carriage of such oil cargo is in conformity with the certificate (see also 1.11 of the Record of Construction and Equipment for Oil Tankers).

1.3   Through examining the Record of Construction and Equipment, the PSCO may establish how the ship is equipped for the prevention of marine pollution.

1.4   If the certificate is valid and the general impression and visual observations on board confirm a good standard of maintenance, the PSCO should generally confine the inspection to reported deficiencies, if any.

1.5   If, however, the PSCO, from general impressions or observations on board, has clear grounds for believing that the condition of the ship or its equipment does not correspond substantially with the particulars of the certificate, a more detailed inspection should be initiated.

1.6   The inspection of the engine-room should begin with forming a general impression of the state of the engine-room, the presence of traces of oil in the engine-room bilges and the ship's routine for disposing of oil-contaminated water from the engine-room spaces.

1.7   Next a closer examination of the ship's equipment as listed in the IOPP Certificate may take place. This examination should also confirm that no unapproved modifications have been made to the ship and its equipment.

1.8 Should any doubt arise as to the maintenance or the condition of the ship or its equipment, then further examination and testing may be conducted as considered necessary. In this respect, reference is made to the IMO guidelines for surveys under Annex I of MARPOL 73/78 (resolution MEPC.11(18)).

1.9 The PSCO should bear in mind that a ship may be equipped over and above the requirements of Annex I of MARPOL 73/78. If such equipment is malfunctioning, the flag State should be informed. This alone, however, should not cause a ship to be detained unless the discrepancy presents an unreasonable threat of harm to the marine environment.

1.10 In cases of oil tankers, the inspection should include the cargo tank and pump-room area of the ship and should begin with forming a general impression of the layout of the tanks, the cargoes carried and the routine of cargo slops disposal.

2 Ships of non-parties to the Convention and other ships not required to carry an IOPP Certificate

2.1 As this category of ships is not provided with an IOPP Certificate, the PSCO should be satisfied with regard to the construction and equipment standards relevant to the ship on the basis of the requirements set out in Annex I of MARPOL 73/78.

2.2 In all other respects the PSCO should be guided by the procedures for ships referred to in section 1 above.

2.3 If the ship has some form of certification other than the IOPP Certificate, the PSCO may take the form and content of this documentation into account in the evaluation of that ship.

3 Control

In exercising the control functions, the PSCO should use professional judgement to determine whether to detain the ship until any noted deficiencies are corrected or to allow it to sail with certain deficiencies which do not pose an unreasonable threat of harm to the marine environment. In doing this the PSCO should be guided by the principle that the requirements contained in Annex I of MARPOL 73/78, in respect of construction and equipment and the operation of ships, are essential for the protection of the marine environment and that departure from these requirements could constitute an unreasonable threat of harm to the marine environment.

Part 2
Contravention of discharge provisions

1   Experience has shown that information furnished to the flag State as envisaged in chapter 3 of the present Procedures is often inadequate to enable the flag State to initiate proceedings in respect of the alleged violation of the discharge requirements. This appendix is intended to identify information which is often needed by a flag State for the prosecution of such possible violations.

2   It is recommended that, in preparing a port State report on deficiencies where contravention of the discharge requirements is involved, the authorities of the coastal or port State be guided by the itemized list of possible evidence as shown in part 3 of this appendix. It should be borne in mind in this connection that:

> **.1**   the report aims to provide the optimal collation of obtainable data; however, even if all the information cannot be provided, as much information as possible should be submitted;

> **.2**   it is important for all the information included in the report to be supported by facts which, when considered as a whole, would lead the port or coastal State to believe a contravention had occurred.

3   In addition to the port State report on deficiencies, a report should be completed by a port or coastal State, on the basis of the itemized list of possible evidence. It is important that these reports are supplemented by documents such as:

> **.1**   a statement by the observer of the pollution. In addition to the information required under section 1 of part 3 of this appendix the statement should include considerations which lead the observer to conclude that none of any other possible pollution sources is in fact the source;

> **.2**   statements concerning the sampling procedures both of the slick and on board. These should include location of and time when samples were taken, identity of person(s) taking the samples and receipts identifying the persons having custody and receiving transfer of the samples;

.3   reports of analyses of samples taken of the slick and on board. The reports should include the results of the analyses, a description of the method employed, reference to or copies of scientific documentation attesting to the accuracy and validity of the method employed and names of persons performing the analyses and their experience;

.4   a statement by the PSCO on board together with the PSCO's rank and organization;

.5   statements by persons being questioned;

.6   statements by witnesses;

.7   photographs of the oil slick;

.8   copies of relevant pages of Oil Record Books, log-books, discharge recordings, etc.

All observations, photographs and documentation should be supported by a signed verification of their authenticity. All certifications, authentications or verifications should be executed in accordance with the laws of the State which prepares them. All statements should be signed and dated by the person making the statement and, if possible, by a witness to the signing. The names of the persons signing statements should be printed in legible script above or below the signature.

4   The report referred to under paragraphs 2 and 3 above should be sent to the flag State. If the coastal State observing the pollution and the port State carrying out the investigation on board are not the same, the State carrying out the latter investigation should also send a copy of its findings to the State observing the pollution and requesting the investigation.

Part 3
Itemized list of possible evidence on alleged contravention of the MARPOL 73/78 Annex I discharge provisions

1   **Action on sighting oil pollution**

1.1   *Particulars of ship or ships suspected of contravention*

.1   Name of ship

.2   Reasons for suspecting the ship

.3   Date and time (UTC) of observation or identification

.4 Position of ship

.5 Flag and port of registry

.6 Type (e.g. tanker, cargo ship, passenger ship, fishing vessel), size (estimated tonnage) and other descriptive data (e.g. superstructure colour and funnel mark)

.7 Draught condition (loaded or in ballast)

.8 Approximate course and speed

.9 Position of slick in relation to ship (e.g. astern, port, starboard)

.10 Part of the ship from which side discharge was seen emanating

.11 Whether discharge ceased when ship was observed or contacted by radio

1.2 *Particulars of slick*

.1 Date and time (UTC) of observation if different from 1.1.3

.2 Position of oil slick in longitude and latitude if different from 1.1.4

.3 Approximate distance in nautical miles from the nearest landmark

.4 Approximate overall dimension of oil slick (length, width and percentage thereof covered by oil)

.5 Physical description of oil slick (direction and form, e.g. continuous, in patches or in windrows)

.6 Appearance of oil slick (indicate categories)
- Category A: Barely visible under most favourable light conditions
- Category B: Visible as silvery sheen on water surface
- Category C: First trace of colour may be observed
- Category D: Bright band of colour
- Category E: Colours begin to turn dull
- Category F: Colours are much darker

.7 Sky conditions (bright sunshine, overcast, etc.), lightfall and visibility (kilometres) at the time of observation

.8 Sea state

.9 Direction and speed of surface wind

.10 Direction and speed of current

1.3 *Identification of the observer(s)*

   .1 Name of the observer

   .2 Organization with which observer is affiliated (if any)

   .3 Observer's status within the organization

   .4 Observation made from aircraft/ship/shore/otherwise

   .5 Name or identity of ship or aircraft from which the observation was made

   .6 Specific location of ship, aircraft, place on shore or otherwise from which observation was made

   .7 Activity engaged in by observer when observation was made, for example: patrol, voyage, flight (*en route* from . . . . to . . . .), etc.

1.4 *Method of observation and documentation*

   .1 Visual

   .2 Conventional photographs

   .3 Remote sensing records and/or remote sensing photographs

   .4 Samples taken from slick

   .5 Any other form of observation (specify)

   Note: A photograph of the discharge should preferably be in colour. Photographs can provide the following information: that a material on the sea surface is oil; that the quantity of oil discharged does constitute a violation of the Convention; that the oil is being, or has been, discharged from a particular ship; and the identity of the ship.

   Experience has shown that the aforementioned can be obtained with the following three photographs:

     – details of the slick taken almost vertically down from an altitude of less than 300 m with the sun behind the photographer;

     – an overall view of the ship and "slick" showing oil emanating from a particular ship; and

     – details of the ship for the purposes of identification.

1.5 *Other information if radio contact can be established*

   .1 Master informed of pollution

   .2 Explanation of master

.3   Ship's last port of call

.4   Ship's next port of call

.5   Name of ship's master and owner

.6   Ship's call sign

2   **Investigation on board**

2.1   *Inspection of IOPP Certificate*

    .1   Name of ship

    .2   Distinctive number or letters

    .3   Port of registry

    .4   Type of ship

    .5   Date and place of issue

    .6   Date and place of endorsement

Note: If the ship is not issued an IOPP Certificate, as much as possible of the requested information should be given.

2.2   *Inspection of supplement of the IOPP Certificate*

    .1   Applicable paragraphs of sections 2, 3, 4, 5 and 6 of the supplement (non-oil tankers)

    .2   Applicable paragraphs of sections 2, 3, 4, 5, 6, 7, 8, 9 and 10 of the supplement (oil tankers)

Note: If the ship does not have an IOPP Certificate, a description should be given of the equipment and arrangements on board, designed to prevent marine pollution.

2.3   *Inspection of Oil Record Book (ORB)*

    .1   Copy sufficient pages of the ORB – part I to cover a period of 30 days prior to the reported incident

    .2   Copy sufficient pages of the ORB – part II (if on board) to cover a full loading/unloading/ballasting and tank cleaning cycle of the ship. Also copy the tank diagram

2.4   *Inspection of log-book*

    .1   Last port, date of departure, draught forward and aft

    .2   Current port, date of arrival, draught forward and aft

    .3   Ship's position at or near the time the incident was reported

.4 Spot check if positions mentioned in the log-book agree with positions noted in the ORB

2.5 *Inspection of other documentation on board*

Other documentation relevant for evidence (if necessary, make copies) such as:

— recent ullage sheets
— records of monitoring and control equipment

2.6 *Inspection of ship*

.1 Ship's equipment in accordance with the supplement of the IOPP Certificate

.2 Samples taken. State location on board

.3 Traces of oil in vicinity of overboard discharge outlets

.4 Condition of engine-room and contents of bilges

.5 Condition of oily water separator, filtering equipment and alarm, stopping or monitoring arrangements

.6 Contents of sludge and/or holding tanks

.7 Sources of considerable leakage

On oil tankers, the following additional evidence may be pertinent:

.8 Oil on surface of segregated or dedicated clean ballast

.9 Condition of pump-room bilges

.10 Condition of COW system

.11 Condition of IG system

.12 Condition of monitoring and control system

.13 Slop tank contents (estimate quantity of water and of oil)

2.7 *Statements of persons concerned*

If the ORB – part I has not been properly completed, information on the following questions may be pertinent:

.1 Was there a discharge (accidental or intentional) at the time indicated on the incident report?

.2 Is the bilge discharge controlled automatically?

.3 If so, at what time was this system last put into operation and at what time was this system last put on manual mode?

.4   If not, what were date and time of the last bilge discharge?

.5   What was the date of the last disposal of residue and how was disposal effected?

.6   Is it usual to effect discharge of bilge water directly to the sea, or to store bilge water first in a collecting tank? Identify the collecting tank

.7   Have oil fuel tanks recently been used as ballast tanks?

If the ORB – part II has not been properly completed, information on the following questions may be pertinent:

.8   What was the cargo/ballast distribution in the ship on departure from the last port?

.9   What was the cargo/ballast distribution in the ship on arrival in the current port?

.10   When and where was the last loading effected?

.11   When and where was the last unloading effected?

.12   When and where was the last discharge of dirty ballast?

.13   When and where was the last cleaning of cargo tanks?

.14   When and where was the last COW operation and which tanks were washed?

.15   When and where was the last decanting of slop tanks?

.16   What is the ullage in the slop tanks and the corresponding height of interface?

.17   Which tanks contained the dirty ballast during the ballast voyage (if ship arrived in ballast)?

.18   Which tanks contained the clean ballast during the ballast voyage (if ship arrived in ballast)?

In addition, the following information may be pertinent:

.19   Details of the present voyage of the ship (previous ports, next ports, trade)

.20   Contents of oil fuel and ballast tanks

.21   Previous and next bunkering, type of oil fuel

.22 Availability or non-availability of reception facilities for oily wastes during the present voyage

.23 Internal transfer of oil fuel during the present voyage

In the case of oil tankers, the following additional information may be pertinent:

.24 The trade the ship is engaged in, such as short/long distance, crude or product or alternating crude/product, lightering service, oil/dry bulk

.25 Which tanks clean and dirty

.26 Repairs carried out or envisaged in cargo tanks

Miscellaneous information:

.27 Comments in respect of condition of ship's equipment

.28 Comments in respect of pollution report

.29 Other comments

3 Investigation ashore

3.1 *Analyses of oil samples*

Indicate method and results of the samples' analyses

3.2 *Further information*

Additional information on the ship, obtained from oil terminal staff, tank cleaning contractors or shore reception facilities, may be pertinent.

> *Note*: Any information under this heading is, if practicable, to be corroborated by documentation such as signed statements, invoices, receipts, etc.

4 Information not covered by the foregoing

5 Conclusion

5.1 Summing up of the investigator's technical conclusions

5.2 Indication of applicable provisions of Annex I of MARPOL 73/78 which the ship is suspected of having contravened

5.3 Did the results of the investigation warrant the filing of a deficiency report?

Part 4
Guidelines for in-port inspection of crude oil washing procedures

1   Preamble

1.1   Guidelines for the in-port inspection of crude oil washing procedures, as called for by resolution 7 of the International Conference on Tanker Safety and Pollution Prevention, 1978, are required to provide a uniform and effective control of crude oil washing to ensure compliance of ships at all times with the provisions of MARPOL 73/78.

1.2   The design of the crude oil washing installation is subject to the approval of the flag Administration. However, although the operational aspect of crude oil washing is also subject to the approval of the same Administration, it might be necessary for a port State authority to see to it that continuing compliance with agreed procedures and parameters is ensured.

1.3   The COW Operations and Equipment Manual has been so specified that it contains all the necessary information relating to the operation of crude oil washing on a particular tanker. The objectives of the inspection would then be to ensure that the provisions of the Manual dealing with safety procedures and with pollution prevention are being strictly adhered to.

1.4   The method of the inspection is at the discretion of the port State authority and may cover the entire operation or only those parts of the operation which occur when the PSCO is on board.

1.5   Inspection will be governed by articles 5 and 6 of the Convention.

2   Inspections

2.1   A port State should make the appropriate arrangements so as to ensure compliance with requirements governing the crude oil washing of oil tankers. This is not, however, to be construed as relieving terminal operators and ship owners of their obligations to ensure that the operation is undertaken in accordance with the regulations.

2.2   The inspection may cover the entire operation of crude oil washing or only certain aspects of it. It is thus in the interest of all concerned that the ship's records with regard to the COW operations are maintained at all times so that a PSCO may verify those operations undertaken prior to the inspection.

3 Ship's personnel

3.1 The person in charge and the other nominated persons who have responsibility in respect of the crude oil washing operation should be identified. They must, if required, be able to show that their qualifications meet the requirements as appropriate of 5.2 and 5.3 of the revised specifications for the design, operation and control of crude oil washing systems (resolution A.446(XI)).

3.2 The verification may be accomplished by reference to the individual's discharge papers, testimonials issued by the ship's operator or by certificates issued by a training centre approved by an Administration. The numbers of such personnel should be at least as stated in the Manual.

4 Documentation

4.1 The following documents should be available for inspection:

- .1 the IOPP Certificate and the Record of Construction and Equipment, to determine:
- .1.1 whether the ship is fitted with a crude oil washing system as required in regulation 13(6) or (8) of Annex I of MARPOL 73/78;
- .1.2 whether the crude oil washing system is according to and complying with the requirements of regulation 13(B) of Annex I of MARPOL 73/78;
- .1.3 the validity and date of the Operations and Equipment Manual; and
- .1.4 the validity of the Certificate.
- .2 the approved Manual;
- .3 the Oil Record Book; and
- .4 the Cargo Ship Safety Equipment Certificate to confirm that the inert gas system conforms to regulations contained in chapter II-2 of SOLAS 74, as amended.

5 Inert gas system

5.1 Inert gas system regulations require that instrumentation should be fitted for continuously indicating and permanently recording, at all times when inert gas is being supplied, the pressure and the oxygen content of the gas in the inert gas supply main. Reference to the permanent recorder would indicate if the system had been operating before and during the cargo discharge in a satisfactory manner.

5.2   If conditions specified in the Manual are not being met then the washing must be stopped until satisfactory conditions are restored.

5.3   As a further precautionary measure, the oxygen level in each tank to be washed is to be determined at the tank. The meters used should be calibrated and inspected to ensure that they are in good working order. Readings from tanks already washed in port prior to inspection should be available for checking. Spot checks on readings may be instituted.

6   Electrostatic generation

It should be confirmed either from the cargo log or by questioning the person in charge that presence of water in the crude oil is being minimized as required by 6.7 of the revised Specifications (resolution A.446(XI)).

7   Communication

It should be established that effective means of communication exist between the person in charge and the other persons concerned with the COW operation.

8   Leakage on deck

PSCOs should ensure that the COW piping system has been operationally tested for leakage before cargo discharge and that the test has been noted in the ship's Oil Record Book.

9   Exclusion of oil from engine-room

It should be ascertained that the method of excluding cargo oil from the machinery space is being maintained by inspecting the isolating arrangements of the tank washing heater (if fitted) or of any part of the tank washing system which enters the machinery space.

10   Suitability of the crude oil

In judging the suitability of the oil for crude oil washing, the guidance and criteria contained in section 9 of the COW Operations and Equipment Manual should be taken into account.

11 Checklist

It should be determined from the ship's records that the pre-crude oil wash operational checklist was carried out and all instruments functioned correctly. Spot checks on certain items may be instituted.

12 Wash programmes

12.1 Where the tanker is engaged in a multiple port discharge, the Oil Record Book would indicate if tanks were crude oil washed at previous discharge ports or at sea. It should be determined that all tanks which will, or may, be used to contain ballast on the forthcoming voyage will be crude oil washed before the ship departs from the port. There is no obligation to wash any tank other than ballast tanks at a discharge port except that each of these other tanks must be washed at least in accordance with 6.1 of the revised specifications (resolution A.446(XI)). The Oil Record Book should be inspected to check that this is being complied with.

12.2 All crude oil washing must be completed before a ship leaves its final port of discharge.

12.3 If tanks are not being washed in one of the preferred orders given in the Manual, the PSCO should determine that the reason for this, and the proposed order of tank washing, are acceptable.

12.4 For each tank being washed, it should be ensured that the operation is in accordance with the Manual in that:

.1   the deck-mounted machines and the submerged machines are operating either by reference to indicators, the sound patterns or other approved methods;

.2   the deck-mounted machines, where applicable, are programmed as stated;

.3   the duration of the wash is as required; and

.4   the number of tank washing machines being used simultaneously does not exceed that specified.

13 Stripping of tanks

13.1 The minimum trim conditions and the parameters of the stripping operations are to be stated in the Manual.

13.2 All tanks which have been crude oil washed are to be stripped. The adequacy of the stripping is to be checked by hand dipping at least in the aftermost hand dipping location in each tank or by such other means as provided and described in the Manual. It should be ascertained that the adequacy of stripping has been checked or will be checked before the ship leaves its final port of discharge.

14 Ballasting

14.1 Tanks that were crude oil washed at sea will be recorded in the Oil Record Book. These tanks must be left empty between discharge ports for inspection at the next discharge port. Where these tanks are the designated departure ballast tanks they may be required to be ballasted at a very early stage of the discharge. This is for operational reasons and also because they must be ballasted during cargo discharge if hydrocarbon emission is to be contained on the ship. If these tanks are to be inspected when empty, then this must be done shortly after the tanker berths. If a PSCO arrives after the tanks have begun accepting ballast, then the sounding of the tank bottom would not be available. However, an examination of the surface of the ballast water is then possible. The thickness of the oil film should not be greater than that specified in 4.2.10(b) of the revised specifications (resolution A.446(XI)).

14.2 The tanks that are designated ballast tanks will be listed in the Manual. It is, however, left to the discretion of the master or responsible officer to decide which tanks may be used for ballast on the forthcoming voyage. It should be determined from the Oil Record Book that all such tanks have been washed before the tanker leaves its last discharge port. It should be noted that, where a tanker back-loads a cargo of crude oil at an intermediate port into tanks designated for ballast, then it should not be required to wash those tanks at that particular port but at a subsequent port.

14.3 It should be determined from the Oil Record Book that additional ballast water has not been put into tanks which had not been crude oil washed during previous voyages.

14.4 It should be verified that the departure ballast tanks are stripped as completely as possible. Where departure ballast is filled through cargo lines and pumps these must be stripped either into another cargo tank or ashore by the special small diameter line provided for this purpose.

14.5 The methods to avoid vapour emission, where locally required, will be provided in the Manual and they must be adhered to. The PSCO should ensure that this is being complied with.

14.6 The typical procedures for ballasting listed in the Manual must be observed. The PSCO should ensure this is being complied with.

14.7 When departure ballast is to be shifted, the discharge into the sea must be in compliance with regulation 9 of Annex I of MARPOL 73/78. The Oil Record Book should be inspected to ensure that the ship is complying with this.

Appendix 3
Guidelines for investigations and inspections carried out under Annex II of MARPOL 73/78

Part 1
Inspection of certificate (COF or NLS Certificate), ship and equipment

1   Ships required to hold a Certificate

1.1   On boarding and after introducing oneself to the master or responsible ship's officer, the PSCO should examine the Certificate of Fitness, NLS Certificate and Cargo Record Book.

1.2   The Certificate includes information on the type of ship, the dates of surveys and a list of the products which the ship is permitted to carry.

1.3   As a preliminary check, the Certificate's validity should be confirmed by verifying that the Certificate is properly completed and signed and that required surveys have been performed. In reviewing the Certificate, particular attention should be given to verifying that only those noxious liquid substances which are listed on the Certificate are carried and that these substances are in tanks approved for their carriage.

1.4   The Cargo Record Book should be inspected to ensure that the records are up to date. The book should show if the ship left the previous port(s) with residues of noxious liquid substances on board which could not be discharged into the sea. The book could also have relevant entries from the appropriate authorities in the previous ports. If the examination reveals that the ship was permitted to sail from its last unloading port under certain conditions, the PSCO should ascertain that such conditions have been or will be adhered to. If the PSCO discovers an operational violation in this respect, the flag State should be informed by means of a deficiency report.

1.5   If the Certificate is valid and the PSCO's general impressions and visual observations on board confirm a good standard of maintenance, the PSCO should, provided that the Cargo Record Book entries do not show any operational violations, confine the inspection to reported deficiencies, if any.

1.6 If, however, the PSCO's general impressions or observations on board show clear grounds for believing that the condition of the ship, its equipment, or its cargo and slops handling operations do not correspond substantially with the particulars of the Certificate, the PSCO should proceed to a more detailed inspection:

    .1   initially this requires an examination of the ship's approved Procedures and Arrangements Manual (P and A Manual);

    .2   the more detailed inspection should include the cargo and pump-room areas of the ship and should begin with forming a general impression of the layout of the tanks, the cargoes carried, pumping and stripping conditions and cargo;

    .3   next a closer examination of the ship's equipment as shown in the P and A Manual may take place. This examination should also confirm that no unapproved modifications have been made to the ship and its equipment; and

    .4   should any doubt arise as to the maintenance or the condition of the ship or its equipment, then further examination and testing may be conducted as may be necessary. In this respect, reference is made to the IMO guidelines for surveys (resolution MEPC.25(23) and resolution A.560(14)), as appropriate.

1.7 The PSCO should bear in mind that a ship may be equipped over and above the requirements of Annex II of MARPOL 73/78. If such equipment is malfunctioning, the flag State should be informed. This alone, however, should not cause a ship to be detained unless the malfunction presents an unreasonable threat of harm to the marine environment.

2   Ships of non-Parties to the Convention

2.1 As this category of ship is not provided with a COF or NLS Certificate as required by Annex II of MARPOL 73/78, the PSCO should be satisfied with regard to the construction and equipment standards relevant to the ship on the basis of the requirements set out in Annex II of MARPOL 73/78 and the Standards for Procedures and Arrangements.

2.2 In all other respects the PSCO should be guided by the procedures for ships referred to in section 1 above (i.e. Ships required to hold a Certificate).

2.3 If the ship has some form of certification other than the required Certificate, the PSCO may take the form and content of this document into account in the evaluation of that ship. Such a form of certification, however, is only of value to the PSCO if the ship has been provided with a P and A Manual.

3   Control

In exercising the control functions, the PSCO should use professional judgement to determine whether to detain the ship until any noted deficiencies are rectified or to allow it to sail with certain deficiencies which do not pose an unreasonable threat of harm to the marine environment. In doing this, the PSCO should be guided by the principle that the requirements contained in Annex II of MARPOL 73/78 and the Standards for Procedures and Arrangements, in respect of construction and equipment and the operation of ships, are essential for the protection of the marine environment and that departure from these requirements could constitute an unreasonable threat of harm to the marine environment.

Part 2
Contravention of discharge provisions

1   With illegal discharges under Annex I of MARPOL 73/78, past experience has shown that information furnished to the flag State is often inadequate to enable the flag State to cause proceedings to be brought in respect of the alleged violation of the discharge requirements. This appendix is intended to identify information which will be needed by a flag State for the prosecution of violations of the discharge provisions under Annex II of MARPOL 73/78.

2   It is recommended that, in preparing a port State report on deficiencies, where contravention of the discharge requirements is involved, the authorities of a coastal or port State should be guided by the itemized list of possible evidence as shown in part 3 of this appendix. It should be borne in mind in this connection that:

> **.1**   the report aims to provide the optimal collation of obtainable data; however, even if all the information cannot be provided, as much information as possible should be submitted; and
>
> **.2**   it is important for all the information included in the report to be supported by facts which, when considered as a whole, would lead the port or coastal State to believe a contravention has occurred; and

.3   the discharge may have been oil, in which case annex 2 to appendix II of Annex I of MARPOL 73/78 (Control Procedures) applies.

3   In addition to the port State report on deficiencies, a report should be completed by a port or coastal State, on the basis of the itemized list of possible evidence. It is important that these reports are supplemented by documents such as:

.1   a statement by the observer of the pollution. In addition to the information required under section 1 of part 3 of this appendix, the statement should include considerations which have led the observer to conclude that none of any other possible pollution sources is in fact the source;

.2   statements concerning the sampling procedures both of the slick and on board. These include location of and time when samples were taken, identity of person(s) taking the samples and receipts identifying the persons having custody and receiving transfer of the samples;

.3   reports of analyses of samples taken of the slick and on board; the reports should include the results of the analyses, a description of the method employed, reference to or copies of scientific documentation attesting to the accuracy and validity of the method employed and names of persons performing the analyses and their experience;

.4   a statement by the PSCO on board together with the PSCO's rank and organization;

.5   statements by persons being questioned;

.6   statements by witnesses;

.7   photographs of the slick; and

.8   copies of relevant pages of the Cargo Record Book, log-books, discharge recordings, etc.

All observations, photographs and documentation should be supported by a signed verification of their authenticity. All certifications, authentications or verifications should be executed in accordance with the laws of the State which prepares them. All statements should be signed and dated by the person making the statement and, if possible, by a witness to the signing. The names of the persons signing statements should be printed in legible script above or below the signature.

4   The report referred to under 2 and 3 should be sent to the flag State. If the coastal State observing the pollution and the port State carrying out the investigation on board are not the same, the State carrying out the latter investigation should also send a copy of its findings to the State observing the pollution and requesting the investigation.

Part 3
Itemized list of possible evidence on alleged contravention of the MARPOL 73/78 Annex II discharge provisions

1   **Action on sighting pollution**

1.1   *Particulars of ship or ships suspected of contravention*

    .1   Name of ship

    .2   Reasons for suspecting the ship

    .3   Date and time (UTC) of observation or identification

    .4   Position of ship

    .5   Flag and port of registry

    .6   Type, size (estimated tonnage) and other descriptive data (e.g. superstructure colour and funnel mark)

    .7   Draught condition (loaded or in ballast)

    .8   Approximate course and speed

    .9   Position of slick in relation to ship (e.g. astern, port, starboard)

    .10   Part of the ship from which discharge was seen emanating

    .11   Whether discharge ceased when ship was observed or contacted by radio

1.2   *Particulars of slick*

    .1   Date and time (UTC) of observation if different from 1.1.3

    .2   Position of slick in longitude and latitude if different from 1.1.4

    .3   Approximate distance in nautical miles from the nearest land

    .4   Depth of water according to sea chart

    .5   Approximate overall dimension of slick (length, width and percentage thereof covered)

.6 Physical description of slick (direction and form, e.g. continuous, in patches or in windrows)

.7 Colour of slick

.8 Sky conditions (bright sunshine, overcast, etc.), lightfall and visibility (km) at the time of observation

.9 Sea state

.10 Direction and speed of surface wind

.11 Direction and speed of current

1.3 *Identification of the observer(s)*

.1 Name of the observer

.2 Organization with which observer is affiliated (if any)

.3 Observer's status within the organization

.4 Observation made from aircraft (ship) (shore) or otherwise

.5 Name or identity of ship or aircraft from which the observation was made

.6 Specific location of ship, aircraft, place on shore or otherwise from which observation was made

.7 Activity engaged in by observer when observation was made, for example: patrol, voyage, flight (*en route* from ... to ...), etc.

1.4 *Method of observation and documentation*

.1 Visual

.2 Conventional photographs

.3 Remote sensing records and/or remote sensing photographs

.4 Samples taken from slick

.5 Any other form of observation (specify)

Note: A photograph of the discharge should preferably be in colour. The best results may be obtained with the following three photographs:

– details of the slick taken almost vertically down from an altitude of less than 300 m with the sun behind the photographer;

– an overall view of the ship and "slick" showing a substance emanating from the particular ship; and

– details of the ship for the purposes of identification

1.5 *Other information if radio contact can be established*

    .1 Master informed of pollution

    .2 Explanation of master

    .3 Ship's last port of call

    .4 Ship's next port of call

    .5 Name of ship's master and owner

    .6 Ship's call sign

2 **Investigation on board**

2.1 *Inspection of the Certificate (COF or NLS Certificate)*

    .1 Name of ship

    .2 Distinctive number or letters

    .3 Port of registry

    .4 Type of ship

    .5 Date and place of issue

    .6 Date and place of endorsement

2.2 *Inspection of P and A Manual*

    .1 List of Annex II substances the ship is permitted to carry

    .2 Limitations as to tanks in which these substances may be carried

    .3 Ship equipped with an efficient stripping system

    .4 Residue quantities established at survey

2.3 *Inspection of Cargo Record Book (CRB)*

Copy sufficient pages of the CRB to cover a full loading/unloading/ballasting and tank cleaning cycle of the ship. Also copy the tank diagram

2.4 *Inspection of log-book*

    .1 Last port, date of departure, draught forward and aft

    .2 Current port, date of arrival, draught forward and aft

    .3 Ship's position at or near the time the incident was reported

.4 Spot check if times entered in the Cargo Record Book in respect of discharges correspond with sufficient distance from the nearest land, the required ship's speed and with sufficient water depth

2.5 *Inspection of other documentation on board*

Other documentation relevant for evidence (if necessary, make copies) such as:

— cargo documents of cargo presently or recently carried, together with relevant information on required unloading temperature, viscosity and/or melting point

— records of temperature of substances during unloading

— records of monitoring equipment if fitted

2.6 *Inspection of ship*

.1 Ship's equipment in accordance with the P and A Manual

.2 Samples taken; state location on board

.3 Sources of considerable leakage

.4 Cargo residues on surface of segregated or dedicated clean ballast

.5 Condition of pump-room bilges

.6 Condition of monitoring system

.7 Slop tank contents (estimate quantity of water and residues)

2.7 *Statements of persons concerned*

If the CRB has not been properly completed, information on the following questions may be pertinent:

.1 Was there a discharge (accidental or intentional) at the time indicated on the incident report?

.2 Which tanks are going to be loaded in the port?

.3 Which tanks needed cleaning at sea? Had the tanks been prewashed?

.4 When and where were these cleaned?

.5 Residues of which substances were involved?

.6 What was done with the tank washing slops?

.7   Was the slop tank, or cargo tank used as a slop tank, discharged at sea?

.8   When and where was the discharge effected?

.9   What are the contents of the slop tank or cargo tank used as slop tank?

.10 Which tanks contained the dirty ballast during the ballast voyage (if ship arrived in ballast)?

.11 Which tanks contained the clean ballast during the ballast voyage (if ship arrived in ballast)?

.12 Details of the present voyage of the ship (previous ports, next ports, trade)

.13 Difficulties experienced with discharge to shore reception facilities

.14 Difficulties experienced with efficient stripping operations

.15 Which tanks are clean or dirty on arrival?

.16 Repairs carried out or envisaged in cargo tanks

Miscellaneous information

.17 Comments in respect of condition of ship's equipment

.18 Comments in respect of pollution report

.19 Other comments.

3   **Investigation ashore**

3.1   *Analyses of samples*

Indicate method and results of the samples' analyses.

3.2   *Further information*

Additional information on the ship, obtained from terminal staff, tank cleaning contractors or shore reception facilities may be pertinent

Note: Any information under this heading is, if practicable, to be corroborated by documentation such as signed statements, invoices, receipts, etc.

3.3 *Information from previous unloading port terminal*

    .1   Confirmation that the ship unloaded, stripped or prewashed in accordance with its P and A Manual

    .2   The nature of difficulties, if any

    .3   Restrictions by authorities under which the ship was permitted to sail

    .4   Restrictions in respect of shore reception facilities

4   **Information not covered by the foregoing**

5   **Conclusion**

    .1   Summing up of the investigator's conclusions

    .2   Indication of applicable provisions of Annex II of MARPOL 73/78 which the ship is suspected of having contravened

    .3   Did the results of the investigation warrant the filing of a deficiency report?

Part 4

Procedures for inspection of unloading, stripping and prewashing operations (mainly in unloading ports)

1   **Introduction**

The PSCO or the surveyor authorized by the Administration exercising control in accordance with regulation 8 of Annex II of MARPOL 73/78 should be thoroughly acquainted with Annex II of MARPOL 73/78 and the custom of the port as of relevance to cargo handling, tank washing, cleaning berths, prohibition of lighters alongside, etc.

2   **Documentation**

2.1   The documentation required for the inspection referred to in this appendix consists of:

    .1   COF or NLS Certificate;

    .2   cargo plan and shipping document;

    .3   Procedures and Arrangements (P and A) Manual; and

    .4   Cargo Record Book.

3 Information by ship's staff

3.1 Of relevance to the PSCO or the surveyor authorized by the Administration is the following:

.1 the intended loading and unloading programme of the ship;

.2 whether unloading and stripping operations can be effected in accordance with the P and A Manual and, if not, the reason why it cannot be done;

.3 the constraints, if any, under which the efficient stripping system operates (i.e. back pressure, ambient air temperature, malfunctioning, etc.);

.4 whether the ship proceeds to, remains inside, or leaves a Special Area; and

.5 whether the ship requests an exemption from the prewashing and the discharge of residues in the unloading port.

3.2 When tank washing is required without the use of water, the PSCO or the surveyor authorized by the Administration is to be informed about the tank washing procedure and disposal of residues.

3.3 When the Cargo Record Book is not up to date, any information on prewash and residue disposal operations outstanding should be supplied.

4 Information from terminal staff

Terminal staff should supply information on limitations imposed upon the ship in respect of back pressure and/or reception facilities.

5 Control

5.1 On boarding and introduction to the master or responsible ship's officer, the PSCO or the surveyor authorized by the Administration should examine the necessary documentation.

5.2 The documentation may be used to establish the following:

.1 noxious liquid substances to be unloaded, their categories and stowage (cargo plan, P and A Manual);

.2 details (possibilities and limitations) of efficient stripping system, if fitted (P and A Manual);

.3 tanks which require prewashing with disposal of tank washings to reception facilities (shipping document and cargo temperature);

.4 tanks which require prewashing with disposal of tank washings either to reception facilities or into the sea (P and A Manual, shipping document and cargo temperature);

.5 prewash operations and/or residue disposal operations outstanding (Cargo Record Book); and

.6 tanks which may not be washed with water due to the nature of substances involved (P and A Manual).

5.3 In respect of the prewash operations referred to under 5.2, the following information is of relevance (P and A Manual):

.1 pressure required for tank washing machines;

.2 duration of one cycle of the tank washing machine and quantity of water used;

.3 washing programmes for the substances involved;

.4 required temperature of washing water; and

.5 special procedures.

5.4 The PSCO or the surveyor authorized by the Administration, in accordance with regulation 8 of Annex II of MARPOL 73/78, should ascertain that unloading, stripping and/or prewash operations are carried out in conformance with the information obtained in accordance with paragraph 2 (Documentation) of this Part. If this cannot be achieved, alternative measures should be taken to ensure that the ship does not proceed to sea with more than the quantities of residue specified in regulation 5A to Annex II of MARPOL 73/78, as applicable. If the residue quantities cannot be reduced by alternative measures, the PSCO or the surveyor authorized by the Administration should inform the port State Administration.

5.5 Care should be taken to ensure that cargo hoses and piping systems of the terminal are not drained back to the ship.

5.6 If a ship is exempted from certain pumping efficiency requirements under regulation 5A to Annex II of MARPOL 73/78 or requests an exemption from certain stripping or prewashing procedures under regulation 8 to Annex II of MARPOL 73/78, the conditions for such exemption set out in the said regulations should be observed. These concern:

.1 regulation 5A(6): the ship is constructed before 1 July 1986 and is exempted from the requirement for reducing its residue quantities to specified limits (i.e. category B substances 0.3 m^3 or 1 m^3 and category C substances 0.9 m^3 or 3 m^3). Whenever a cargo tank is to be washed or ballasted, a prewash is required with disposal of prewash slops to shore reception facilities. The COF or NLS Certificate should have been endorsed to the effect that the ship is solely engaged in restricted voyages;

.2 regulation 5A(7): the ship is never required to ballast its cargo tanks and tank washing is only required for repair or drydocking. The COF or NLS Certificate should indicate the particulars of the exemption. Each cargo tank should be certified for the carriage of only one named substance;

.3 regulations 8(2)(b)(i), 8(5)(b)(i), 8(6)(c)(i) and 8(7)(c)(i): cargo tanks will not be washed or ballasted prior to the next loading;

.4 regulations 8(2)(b)(ii), 8(5)(b)(ii), 8(6)(c)(ii) and 8(7)(c)(ii): cargo tanks will be washed and prewash slops will be discharged to reception facilities in another port. It should be confirmed, in writing, that an adequate reception facility is available at that port for such purpose; and

.5 regulations 8(2)(b)(iii), 8(5)(b)(iii), 8(6)(c)(iii) and 8(7)(c)(iii): the cargo residues can be removed by ventilation.

5.7   The PSCO or the surveyor authorized by the Administration must endorse the Cargo Record Book under section J whenever an exemption referred to under in paragraphs 5.6.3, 5.6.4, and 5.6.5 above has been granted, or whenever a tank, having unloaded category A substances, has been prewashed in accordance with the P and A Manual.

5.8   Alternatively, for category A substances, regulation 8(3) of Annex II of MARPOL 73/78, residual concentration should be measured by the procedures which each port State authorizes. In this case the PSCO or the surveyor authorized by the Administration must endorse in the Cargo Record Book under section K whenever the required residual concentration has been achieved.

5.9   In addition to paragraph 5.7 above, the PSCO or the surveyor authorized by the Administration should endorse the Cargo Record Book whenever the unloading, stripping or prewash of category B, C and D substances, in accordance with the P and A Manual, has actually been witnessed.

5.10   The PSCO or the surveyor authorized by the Administration must be aware that certain "oil-like" noxious liquid substances may be carried on product carriers. Such substances should be indicated on the IOPP Certificate. For the control of ships carrying such substances, the Control

Procedures under Annex I of MARPOL 73/78 apply. The PSCO or the surveyor authorized by the Administration exercising control in accordance with regulation 8 of Annex II of MARPOL 73/78 should be thoroughly acquainted with Annex I of MARPOL 73/78.

Appendix 4
List of certificates and documents

List of certificates and documents which, to the extent applicable, should be checked during the inspection referred to in paragraph 2.2.3 of the Procedures:

1   International Tonnage Certificate (1969);

2   Passenger Ship Safety Certificate;

3   Cargo Ship Safety Construction Certificate;

4   Cargo Ship Safety Equipment Certificate;

5   Cargo Ship Safety Radio Certificate;

6   Exemption Certificate;

7   Cargo Ship Safety Certificate;

8   Document of Compliance (SOLAS 74, regulation II-2/54);

9   Dangerous Goods Special List or Manifest, or Detailed Stowage Plan;

10   International Certificate of Fitness for the Carriage of Liquefied Gases in Bulk, or the Certificate of Fitness for the Carriage of Liquefied Gases in Bulk, whichever is appropriate;

11   International Certificate of Fitness for the Carriage of Dangerous Chemicals in Bulk, or the Certificate of Fitness for the Carriage of Dangerous Chemicals in Bulk, whichever is appropriate;

12   International Oil Pollution Prevention Certificate;

13   International Pollution Prevention Certificate for the Carriage of Noxious Liquid Substances in Bulk;

14   International Load Line Certificate (1966);

15   International Load Line Exemption Certificate;

16   Oil Record Book, parts I and II;

17   Shipboard Oil Pollution Emergency Plan;

18   Cargo Record Book;

19   Minimum Safe Manning Document;

20   Certificates of Competency;

21   Medical certificates (see ILO Convention No. 73);

22   Stability information;

23   Safety Management Certificate and copy of Document of Compliance (SOLAS chapter IX);

24   Certificates as to the ship's hull strength and machinery installations issued by the classification society in question (only to be required if the ship maintains its class with a classification society);

25   Survey Report Files (in case of bulk carriers or oil tankers in accordance with resolution A.744(18));

26   For ro–ro passenger ships, information on the A/A_{max} ratio;

27   Document of authorization for the carriage of grain;

28   Special Purpose Ship Safety Certificate;

29   High-Speed Craft Safety Certificate and Permit to Operate High-Speed Craft;

30   Mobile Offshore Drilling Unit Safety Certificate;

31   For oil tankers, the record of the oil discharge monitoring and control system for the last ballast voyage;

32   The muster list, fire control plan, and, for passenger ships, a damage control plan;

33   Ship's log-book with respect to the records of tests and drills and the log for records of inspection and maintenance of life-saving appliances and arrangements;

34   Procedures and Arrangements Manual (chemical tankers);

35   Cargo Securing Manual;

36   Certificate of Registry or other document of nationality;

37   Garbage Management Plan;

38   Garbage Record Book;

39   Bulk carrier booklet (SOLAS chapter VI regulation 7); and

40   Reports of previous port State control inspections.

Appendix 4A
Guidelines for port State control under the 1969 Tonnage Convention

1   The International Convention on Tonnage Measurement of Ships, 1969, which came into force on 18 July 1982, applies to:

    .1   new ships, i.e. ships the keels of which were laid on or after 18 July 1982; and

    .2   existing ships, i.e. ships the keels of which were laid before 18 July 1982, as from 18 July 1994,

except that, for the purpose of application of SOLAS, MARPOL and STCW Conventions, the interim schemes indicated in paragraph 2 below may apply.

2   In accordance with the interim schemes adopted by the Organization*, the Administration may, at the request of the shipowner, use the gross tonnage determined in accordance with national rules prior to the coming into force of the 1969 Tonnage Convention, for the following ships:

2.1   for the purpose of SOLAS 74:

    .1   ships the keels of which were laid before 1 January 1986;

    .2   in respect of regulation IV/3 of SOLAS 74, ships the keels of which were laid on or after 1 January 1986 but before 18 July 1994; and

    .3   cargo ships of less than 1,600 tons gross tonnage (as determined under the national tonnage rules) the keels of which were laid on or after 1 January 1986 but before 18 July 1994;

2.2   for the purpose of STCW 78, ships falling under the categories of paragraphs 2.1.1 and 2.1.3 above, except that, for the purpose of 1995 amendments to STCW 78, the interim scheme does not apply (see regulation I/15.3 of the 1995 STCW amendments); and

2.3   for the purpose of MARPOL 73/78, ships of less than 400 tons gross tonnage (as determined under the national tonnage rules) the keels of which were laid before 18 July 1994.

---

* Resolutions A.494(XII) in respect of SOLAS 74, A.540(13) in respect of STCW 78, and A.541(13) in respect of MARPOL 73/78.

3   For ships to which the above interim schemes apply, a statement to the effect that the gross tonnage has been measured in accordance with national tonnage rules should be included in the REMARKS column of the International Tonnage Certificate (1969) and in the footnote to the figure of the gross tonnage in the relevant SOLAS, STCW and MARPOL certificates.

4   The PSCO should take the following actions, as appropriate, when deficiencies are found in relation to the 1969 Tonnage Convention:

　　.1   if a ship does not hold a valid 1969 Tonnage Certificate, a letter of warning should be issued to the master or shipowner;

　　.2   if the required remarks and footnote are not included in the relevant certificates of ships to which the interim schemes apply, this deficiency should be notified to the master;

　　.3   if the main characteristics of the ship differ from those entered in the 1969 International Tonnage Certificate, so as to lead to an increase in the gross tonnage or net tonnage, the flag State should be informed without delay.

5   The control provisions of article 12 of the 1969 Tonnage Convention do not include a provision for detention of ships.

Appendix 5
Report of inspection in accordance with IMO port State control procedures (resolution A.787(19), as amended by resolution A.882(21))*

FORM A

(Reporting authority)   Copy to: Master
(Address)   Head office
(Telephone)   PSCO
(Telefax)

If ship is detained, copy to:
Flag State
IMO
Recognized organization, if applicable

1   Name of reporting authority . . . .

2   Name of ship . . . . **3**   Flag of ship . . . .

4   Type of ship . . . .

5   Call sign . . . . **6**   IMO number . . . .

7   Gross tonnage . . . . **8**   Deadweight (where applicable) . . . . .

9   Year of build . . . . **10**   Date of inspection . . . .

11   Place of inspection . . . . **12**   Classification society . . . .

13   Date of release from detention† . . . .

14   Particulars of company† . . . .

15   Relevant certificate(s)† . . . .

a) Title	b) Issuing authority	c) Dates of issue and expiry
1	. . . .	. . . .
2	. . . .	. . . .
3	. . . .	. . . .
4	. . . .	. . . .
5	. . . .	. . . .
6	. . . .	. . . .

---

* This inspection report has been issued solely for the purposes of informing the master and other port States that an inspection by the port State, mentioned in the heading, has taken place. This inspection report cannot be construed as a seaworthiness certificate *in excess of* the certificate the ship is required to carry.

† To be completed in the event of a detention.

d) Information on last intermediate or annual survey[†]

	Date	Surveying authority	Place
1	. . . .	. . . .	. . . .
2	. . . .	. . . .	. . . .
3	. . . .	. . . .	. . . .
4	. . . .	. . . .	. . . .
5	. . . .	. . . .	. . . .
6	. . . .	. . . .	. . . .

16 Deficiencies ☐ No ☐ yes (see attached FORM B)
17 Ship detained ☐ No ☐ yes[*]
18 Supporting documentation ☐ No ☐ yes (see annex)

Issuing office . . . .   Name . . . .
                                          (duly authorized PSCO of
                                             reporting authority)

Telephone . . . .

Telefax . . . .   Signature . . . .

This report must be retained on board for a period of two years and must be available for consultation by Port State Control Officers at all times.

---

[*] Masters, shipowners and/or operators are advised that detailed information on a detention may be subject to future publication.

[†] To be completed in the event of a detention.

Report of inspection in accordance with IMO port State control procedures (resolution A.787(19), as amended by resolution A.882(21))*

FORM B

(Reporting authority)   Copy to: Master
(Address)   Head office
(Telephone)   PSCO
(Telefax)

If ship is detained, copy to:
                                         Flag State
                                         IMO
                                         Recognized organization (if applicable)

2   Name of ship . . . .   **6** IMO number . . . .

10 Date of inspection . . . .   **11** Place of inspection. . . . .

19 Nature of deficiency[†]	Convention[‡]	**20** Action taken[§]
. . . .	. . . .	. . . .
. . . .	. . . .	. . . .
. . . .	. . . .	. . . .
. . . .	. . . .	. . . .
. . . .	. . . .	. . . .
. . . .	. . . .	. . . .
. . . .	. . . .	. . . .
. . . .	. . . .	. . . .
. . . .	. . . .	. . . .
. . . .	. . . .	. . . .

Name . . . .
(duly authorized PSCO of reporting authority)

Signature . . . .

---

* This inspection report has been issued solely for the purposes of informing the master and other port States that an inspection by the port State, mentioned in the heading, has taken place. This inspection report cannot be construed as a seaworthiness certificate *in excess of* the certificate the ship is required to carry.

† This inspection was not a full survey and deficiencies listed may not be exhaustive. In the event of a detention, it is recommended that a full survey is carried out and all deficiencies are rectified before an application for re-inspection is made.

‡ To be completed in the event of a detention.

§ Actions taken include i.e.: ship detained/released, flag State informed, classification society informed, next port informed.

Appendix 6
Report of deficiencies not fully rectified or only provisionally repaired

In accordance with the provision of paragraph 4.7.3 of IMO port State control procedures (resolution A.787(19), as amended by resolution A.882(21))

(Copy to maritime Authority of next port of call, flag Administration, or other certifying authority as appropriate)

1 From (country/region): . . . . . . **2** Port: . . . .

3 To (country/region): . . . . **4** Port: . . . .

5 Name of ship: . . . . **6** Date departed: . . . .

7 Estimated place and time of arrival: . . . .

8 IMO number: . . . . **9** Flag of ship & POR: . . . .

10 Type of ship: . . . . **11** Call sign: . . . .

12 Gross tonnage: . . . . **13** Year of build: . . . .

14 Issuing authority of relevant certificate(s):

15 Nature of deficiencies to be rectified: **16** Suggested action (including action at next port of call): . . . .

. . . .
. . . .
. . . .
. . . .
. . . .
. . . .
. . . .
. . . .

17 Action taken:

. . . .
. . . .
. . . .

Reporting Authority: . . . .

Office: . . . .

Name: . . . .

(duly authorized PSC officer of reporting authority)

Facsimile: . . . .

Signature: . . . . Date: . . . .

Appendix 7

Report of action taken to the notifying authority

In accordance with the provision of paragraph 4.7.3 of
IMO port State control procedures (resolution A.787(19),
as amended by resolution A.882(21))

(by facsimile and/or mail)

1   To: (Name) . . . .

                        (Position) . . . .

                        (Authority) . . . .

                        Telephone: . . . .   Telefax: . . . .

                        Date:

2   From: (Name) . . . .

                        (Position) . . . .

                        (Authority) . . . .

                        Telephone: . . . .   Telefax: . . . .

3   Name of ship: . . . .

4   Call sign: . . . .   **5**   IMO number: . . . .

6   Port of inspection: . . . .

7   Date of inspection: . . . .

8   Action taken:

      (a)   Deficiencies   (b)   Action taken

. . . .	. . . .
. . . .	. . . .
. . . .	. . . .
. . . .	. . . .
. . . .	. . . .
. . . .	. . . .
. . . .	. . . .
. . . .	. . . .
. . . .	. . . .
. . . .	. . . .

9   Next port: Date:

10   Supporting documentation   ☐ No   ☐ Yes   (*See attached*)

                                    Signature: . . . .

Appendix 8

Report of contravention of
MARPOL 73/78 (article 6)

IMO port State control procedures (resolution A.787(19),
as amended by resolution A.882(21))

(Issuing authority)   Copy to: Master
(Address)
(Telephone)
(Telefax)

1   Reporting country . . . .

2   Name of ship   3   Flag of ship . . . .

4   Type of ship . . . .

5   Call sign   6   IMO number . . . .

7   Gross tonnage   8   Deadweight (where appropriate) . .

9   Year of build   10   Classification society . . . .

11   Date of incident   12   Place of incident . . . .

13   Date of investigation . . . .

14   In case of contravention of discharge provisions, a report may be completed
in addition to port State report on deficiencies. This report should be in
accordance with parts 2 and 3 of appendix 2 and/or parts 2 and 3 of
appendix 3, as applicable, and should be supplemented by documents, such
as:

    .1   a statement by the observer of the pollution;

    .2   the appropriate information listed under section 1 of part 3 of
appendices 2 and 3 to the Procedures; the statement should include
considerations which lead the observer to conclude that none of any
other possible pollution sources is in fact the source;

    .3   statements concerning the sampling procedures both of the slick and
on board. These should include location of and time when samples
were taken, identity of person(s) taking the samples and receipts
identifying the persons having custody and receiving transfer of the
samples;

    .4   reports of analyses of samples taken of the slick and on board; the
reports should include the results of the analyses, a description of the
method employed, reference to or copies of scientific documentation
attesting to the accuracy and validity of the method employed and
names of persons performing the analyses and their experience;

    .5   if applicable, a statement by the PSCO on board together with the
PSCO's rank and organization;

.6   statements by persons being questioned;

.7   statements by witnesses;

.8   photographs of the slick;

.9   copies of relevant pages of Oil/Cargo Record Books, log-books, discharge recordings, etc.

Name and Title (duly authorized contravention investigating official)

. . . .

. . . .

. . . .

. . . .

Signature

Appendix 9
Comments by flag State on deficiency report

Name of ship: _____

IMO number/call sign: _____

Flag State: _____

Gross tonnage: _____

Deadweight (where appropriate): _____

Date of report: _____

Report by: _____

Classification Society or Recognized organization involved:

_____

_____

Brief note on action taken: _____

_____

_____

_____

_____

Appendix 10

Contact addresses of responsible national authorities*
Ships' inspection – Head offices
(including Secretariats of Memoranda of Understanding
on Port State Control)

AUTHORITY Competency	**Competent Administration/Services** Address
ALGERIA Ships inspection – Head office	Directeur de la Marine Marchande 119 rue Didouche Mourad Tel: 213 2 747572 Fax: 213 2 743395/747624/745316
ALBANIA Ships inspection – Head office	Ministère des Transports et Télécommunications Département du Transport Maritime Tirana Tel: 355 42 25862 Fax: 355 42 27773
ANGOLA Ships inspection – Head office	Direção Nacional da Marinha Mercante e Portos Ministério dos Transportes e Comunicações C.P. 2393 Rua Rainha Ginga, No. 74, 4 Andar Luanda Tel: 244 2 339847/8 Fax: 244 2 394296 Telex: 3352 marport an

ANTIGUA AND BARBUDA
As a flag State for
PSC matters
	Department of Marine Services
	   and Merchant Shipping
	Chief Marine Surveyor
	Deepwater Harbour
	P.O. Box 1052
	St. John's
	Antigua W.I.
	Tel: 1 268 462 1273/4353 – 1 268 461 2380
	Fax: 1 268 462 4358
	Email: info@antiguamarine.com
	         www.antiguamarine.com

---

* These details may be changed. For a current list, see the website www.imo.org.

AUTHORITY Competency	Competent Administration/Services Address
ANTIGUA AND BARBUDA Ships inspection – Head office	Department of Marine Services and Merchant Shipping Director and Registrar General P.O. Box 1052 St. John's Antigua W.I. Tel: 1 268 462 1273/4353 Fax: 1 268 462 4358 Email: info@antiguamarine.com www.antiguamarine.com
ARGENTINA Ships inspection – Head office	Prefectura Naval Argentina Prefectura de Zona Mar Argentino Norte Av. Eduardo Madero 235, piso 1 (1106) Buenos Aires C.F. Tel: 541 318 7467 Fax: 541 318 7467
ASIA PACIFIC MOU MoU on PSC information – Manager	Maritime Administration Seaport 3 Nizneportovaya Street Vladivostok, 690090 Russia Tel: 7 4232 510817 Fax: 7 4232 497424 Email: vit@tmou.org, vit@pma.ru
MoU on PSC – Secretary	Tokyo MOU Secretariat Tomoecho Annex Building 6F 3-8-26, Tornamon Minato-ku Tokyo Japan 105-0001 Tel: 81 3 3433 0621 Fax: 81 3 3433 0624 Email: yoshio.sasamura@nifty.ne.jp tmou.okada@nifty.ne.jp
AUSTRALIA Ships inspection – Head office	Marine Surveyor Australian Maritime Safety Authority 25 Constitution Ave Canberra City ACT 2601 G.P.O. Box 2181 CANBERRA ACT 2600 Tel: 61 2 6279 5048 Fax: 61 2 6279 5058 Email: psc@amsa.gov.au

AUTHORITY Competency	Competent Administration/Services Address
AUSTRIA Ships inspection – Head office	Bundesministerium für öffentliche Wirtschaft und Verkehr Oberste Schiffahrtsbehörde Radetzkystrasse 2 A-1030 Vienna Tel: 43 1 71162 5900 Fax: 43 1 71162 5999 Telex: 61-3221155
AZERBAIJAN Ships inspection – Head office	Caspian Shipping Company 5 M.E. Rasul-zade Street Baku 370005 Tel: 994 12 93 20 58/93 46 63 Fax: 994 12 93 53 39 Telex: 142411 KSSC SU 142102 MRF SU
BAHAMAS Ships inspection – Head office	Bahamas Maritime Authority 10 Chesterfield Street London W1X 8AH Tel: 44 20 7 290 1500 Fax: 44 20 7 290 1542
BANGLADESH Ships inspection – Head office	Department of Shipping 1st 12 Storied Building Segun Bagicha Dhaka Tel: 880 2 407643/405434
BARBADOS Ships inspection & casualty investigation – Head office (All foreign-going ships and near-coastal and Caribbean trade ships 150 gross tons and over)	Principal Registrar of Ships Barbados Ships' Registry Barbados High Commission 1 Great Russell Street London WC1B 3JY Tel: 44 20 7 636 5739 Fax: 44 20 7 636 5745
Ships inspection & casualty investigation – Head office (All foreign-going ships and near-coastal and Caribbean trade ships under 150 gross tons)	Director of Maritime Affairs International Transport Division Adriana's Complex Warrens, St. Michael Barbados Tel: 246 425 0034/0072 Fax: 246 425 0101

AUTHORITY Competency	Competent Administration/Services Address
BELGIUM Ships inspection – Head office	Ministère des Communications, Administration des Affaires Maritimes et de la Navigation 104 rue d'Arlon Bruxelles B-1040 Tel: 02 233 1280 Fax: 02 230 1969 Telex: 061+61880 VERTRA B
BELIZE Ships inspection – Head office	International Merchant Marine Registry of Belize Technical Advisor Marina Towers Suite 204, Newtown Barracks Belize City Belize, C.A. Tel: 501 2 35026/35031/35047 Fax: 501 2 35048/35070 Email: immarbe@btl.net
BENIN Ships inspection – Head office	Direction de la Marine Marchande P.O. Box 1234 Cotonou Tel: 229 31 4669/31 5845 Fax: 229 31 3642 Telex: 5225 COBNAM
BLACK SEA MOU MoU on PSC information – Manager	Maritime Administration of Seaport 3 Nizneportovaya Street Vladivostok 690090, Russia Tel: 7 4232 510817 Fax: 7 4232 497424 Email: vit@tmou.org, vit@pma.ru
MoU on PSC – Secretary	Black Sea PSC Interim Secretariat Meclisi Mebusan Cad. No. 18 Salipazari 80040, Istanbul Turkey Tel: 90 212 249 1728 Fax: 90 212 292 5277 Email: kiyi01@superonline.com

AUTHORITY Competency	Competent Administration/Services Address
BOLIVIA Ships inspection – Head office	Bolivian Ships Registry International Maritime Centre 93 Charilaou Trikoupi Str. Kifisia Gr 145–63 Athens Greece Tel: 30 1 80 81180 (4 lines) Fax: 30 1 80 81189 Telex: 218550IMC GR Email: imc@otenet.gr
BRAZIL Ships inspection – Head office	Diretoria de Portos e Costas Rua Teófilo Otoni 4-Centro Rio de Janeiro RJ – Brazil CEP: 20090-070 Tel: 55 21 870 5402 Fax: 55 21 870 5402 Email: secom@dpc.mar.mil.br vina@dpc.mar.mil.br
BRUNEI DARUSSALAM Ships inspection – Head office	Director of Marine Marine Department Muara 4053 Tel: 673 2 771347 to 771356 Fax: 673 2 771357 Telex: MARINE BU 2650
BULGARIA Ships inspection – Head office	Ministry of Transport Chief of the State Inspectorate on Shipping 9 Levski Str. 1000 Sofia Tel: 359 2 88 55 29 Fax: 359 2 88 53 47 Telex: 22208/23209/23200
CAMBODIA Ships inspection – Head office	Office Ministry of Public Works and Transport General Department of Transport Merchant Marine Department Norodom Boulevard Phnom Penh Tel: 855 23 427 862 Fax: 855 23 427 862

AUTHORITY Competency	Competent Administration/Services Address

CAMEROON
Ships inspection –
Head office

Direction de la Marine Marchande
B.P. 416
Douala
Tel: 237 42 89 56/42 03 88
Fax: 237 42 89 56

CANADA
Ships inspection –
Head office
PSC and flag State
contact

Transport Canada, Marine Safety
Place de Ville
Tower C, 11th Floor
330 Sparks Street
Ottawa
Ontario K1A 0N8
Tel: 1 613 991 31 31/990 71 21/911 31 37
Fax: 1 613 993 81 96
Email: pineaub@tc.gc.ca/henderw@tc.gc.ca

CAPE VERDE
Ships inspection –
Head office

Direçao General da Marinha e do Porto
P.O. Box 7
Mindelo
S. Vicente
Tel: 238 324 243
Fax: 238 324 343
Telex: 3032 MARPOR CV

CARIBBEAN MOU
MoU on PSC – Secretary

International Transport Division
Herbert House
Fontabelle
St. Michael
Barbados
Tel: 809 4294156
Fax: 246 4250101

MoU on PSC information –
Manager

Pletterejweg z/n
Willemstad
Curaçao
Netherlands Antilles
Tel: 5999 4611421
Fax: 5999 4612964
Email: sina@curinfo.com
             www.cersis.com/cmic

AUTHORITY Competency	Competent Administration/Services Address
CHILE Ships inspection – Head office	Gobernación Marítima Calle Prat 681 Valparaiso Tel: 56 32 208941 Fax: 56 32 208995 Email: sinav@directemar.cl

CHINA
(PEOPLE'S REPUBLIC
OF)
Ships inspection –
Head office
	Ministry of Communications
	Maritime Safety Administration
	No 11 Jianguomennei Avenue
	Beijing 100736
	Tel: 86 10 529 2246/2213
	           86 10 652 92802
	Fax: 86 10 529 2345
	           86 10 652 92245

COLOMBIA Ships inspection – Head office	Apartado Aéreo No. 20294 Calle 41 #46-20 Edificio DIMAR CAN Santafé de Bogotá D.C. Tel: 57 1 2220247/2220301 Fax: 57 1 2222636 Telex: 44421 DIMAR-CO
COMOROS Ships inspection – Head office	Maritime Administration 28, Schtouri St. (4th Floor) 18537 Piraeus Greece Tel: 301 418 4868 Fax: 301 452 8168 Email: com-reg@hol.gr
CONGO (REPUBLIC OF) Ships inspection – Head office	Direction générale de la Marine Marchande B.P. 1107 Pointe Noire Tel: 242 942 326/940 107 Fax: 242 944 832
CONGO **(THE DEMOCRATIC** **REPUBLIC OF)** Ships inspection – Head office	Directeur de la Marine et des Voies Navigables B.P. 3.144 Kinshasa Gombe

AUTHORITY Competency	Competent Administration/Services Address
COSTA RICA Ships inspection – Head office	Ministerio de Obras Públicas y Transportes P.O. Box 10176 1000 San José Tel: 506 336510/330555 Fax: 506 330605
CÔTE D'IVOIRE Ships inspection – Head office	Directeur des Affaires Maritimes et Portuaires B.P. 67 Abidjan Tel: 225 221 630/215 133 Fax: 225 215 317

CROATIA
Ships inspection –
Head office
	Ministry of Maritime Affairs, Transport
	   and Communications
	Department of Maritime Safety
	10000 Zagreb
	Prisavlje 14
	Tel: 385 1 6169 070
	         385 1 6169 025
	Fax: 385 1 6196 529

CUBA Ships inspection – Head office	Dirección de Inspección y Seguridad Marítima Ministerio de Transporte Boyeros y Tulipan Plaza Ciudad de La Habana Tel: 537 811514/819498 Fax: 537 335118/537 816607
CYPRUS Ships inspection – Head office	Kyllinis Street CY-4007 Mesa Geitonia P. O. Box 6193 CY-3305 Lemesos Tel: 357 5 848100 Fax: 357 5 848200 Telex: 2004 MERSHIPCY Email: dms@cytanet.com.cy
CZECH REPUBLIC Ships inspection – Head office	Ministry of Transport Navigation and Waterways Division Nabrezi L. Svobody 12 11015 Praha 1 Tel: 42 2 23031213/23031151/23031225 Fax: 42 2 24810596

AUTHORITY Competency	Competent Administration/Services Address

DENMARK
Ships inspection –
Head office

Danish Maritime Authority
Vermundsgade 38 C
PO Box 2605
DK-2100 Copenhagen Ø
Tel: 45 39 17 44 00
Fax: 45 39 17 44 01
Telex: 45 31 141 Soefart dk
Email: sfs@dma.dk
            www.sofartsstyrelsen.dk

DJIBOUTI
Ships inspection –
Head office

Ministère des Affaires étrangères et
   de la Coopération
Services des Affaires Maritimes

DOMINICA
Ships inspection –
Head office

Permanent Secretary
Government Headquarters
Roseau
Tel: 1 767 448 4722
             1 767 448 7245
Fax: 809 44 84807
Email: maritime@cwdom.dm

ECUADOR
Ships inspection –
Head office

Dirección General de Intereses Marítimos
Avenida Colon 1370 y Foch
Edificio Salazar Gomez Messanine
Quito
Tel: 593 2 563 075/563 076
Fax: 593 2 563 075
Telex: 22351

EGYPT
Ships inspection –
Head office

Maritime Inspection Department
Ports and Lighthouses Administration
Ras El Tin
Alexandria

EL SALVADOR
Ships inspection –
Head office

Comisión Ejecutiva Portuaria Autónoma (CEPA)
Edificio Torre Roble
Boulevard Los Héroes
P.O. Box 2667
San Salvador
Tel: 503 241133/240881
Fax: 503 241355/529001/399245

AUTHORITY Competency	Competent Administration/Services Address
EQUATORIAL GUINEA Ships inspection – Head office	Ministerio de Communicaciones & Transportes Directorate General of Transports and Civil Aviation Malabo Tel: 240 926 05 Fax: 240 925 15
ERITREA Ships inspection – Head office	Ports and Maritime Transport Authority Head of Technical Services P.O. Box 679 Asmara Tel: 2911 117398/113590/111502 Fax: 2911 113647
ESTONIA Ships inspection – Head office	Estonian National Maritime Board Lasnamäe 48 11413 Tallinn Tel: 372 6205 500 Fax: 372 6205 506
ETHIOPIA Ships inspection – Head office	Ministry of Transport and Communications Head of Maritime Department P.O. 1238 Addis Ababa Tel: 251 1 15 82 27/51 61 66 Ext. 224 Fax: 51 56 65
FIJI Ships inspection – Head office	Fiji Islands Maritime Safety Administration Motibjai Building GPO Box 326 Suva Tel: 679 315 266 Fax: 679 303 251 Email: fimsa@is.com.fj
FINLAND Ships inspection – Head office	Finnish Maritime Administration Porkkalankatu 5 P.O. Box 171 00181 Helsinki Tel: 358 204 48 40 Fax: 358 204 48 4500 Telex: 060+121471 (or 125963) MKH SF Email: www.fma.fi

AUTHORITY Competency	Competent Administration/Services Address
FRANCE As a flag State for PSC matters	Ministère de l'Équipement, des Transports et du Logement Direction des Affaires maritimes et des Gens de mer Bureau du contrôle des navires et des effectifs 3 Place de Fontenoy 75700 Paris Tel: 33 1 44 49 86 41 Fax: 33 1 44 49 86 40 Email: pierre.mitton@equipement.gouv.fr
Ships inspection – Head office	Ministère de l'Équipement, des Transports et du Logement Direction des Affaires maritimes et des Gens de mer Bureau du contrôle des navires et des effectifs 3 Place de Fontenoy 75700 Paris Tel: 33 1 44 49 86 41 Fax: 33 1 44 49 86 40 Telex: 250 823 FPARIS Email: pierre.mitton@equipement.gouv.fr
GABON Ships inspection – Head office	Ministère de la Marine Marchande et de la Pêche Direction Générale de la Marine Marchande B.P. 803 Libreville Tel: 241 760185/760600/745307 Fax: 241 760185/720042
GAMBIA Ships inspection – Head office	Gambia Ports Authority Wellington Street Banjul Tel: 220 227 406 Fax: 220 227 268
GEORGIA Ships inspection – Head office	Maritime Department Maritime Administration 384517 60 Gogebashvili St. Batumi Fax: 99522276202 Telex: 412617 Email: GMA.GOV@batumi.net magheadof@fsc.gov.ge

AUTHORITY Competency	Competent Administration/Services Address
GERMANY Ships inspection – Head office	Bundesministerium für Verkehr Abteilung Seeverkehr Robert–Schuman–Platz 1 P.O. Box 20 01 00 D-53170 Bonn Tel: 49 228 300 4641 Fax: 49 228 300 4609
GHANA Ships inspection – Head office	Ministry of Transport and Communications The Shipping Commissioner Ministry of Roads and Transport Division of Shipping and Navigation P.O. Box M.38 Accra Tel: 233 21663506 Fax: 233 21667114 Telex: 2293
GREECE Ships inspection – Head office	Ministry of Merchant Marine Ocean Shipping Division 150 Grigoriou Lambraki Ave 185 18 Piraeus Tel: 30 1 412 8150/30 1 419 1188 30 1 412 1211 Fax: 30 1 429 1166
GRENADA Ships inspection – Head office	Grenada Ports Authority Burns Point St. George's Tel: 473 440 7678/3031/3439 809 440 3013 Fax: 473 440 3418 809 440 3418 Email: grenport@caribsurf.com
GUINEA Ships inspection – Head office	Direction Nationale de la Marine Marchande Sécurité Maritime et Affaires Portuaires B.P. 06 Conakry Tel: 224 412 743/453 539 Fax: 224 412 604/412 848

AUTHORITY Competency	Competent Administration/Services Address
GUINEA-BISSAU Ships inspection – Head office	Director Nacional de Marinha e Portos C.P. 25 Bissau Tel: 245 201 137
GUYANA Ships inspection – Head office	Ministry of Transport Wight's Lane Kingston Georgetown Tel: 592 2 59350 Fax: 592 2 78545
HAITI Ships inspection – Head office	Service Maritime et de Navigation d'Haiti (SEMANAH) P.O. Box 1563 Boulevard la Saline Port au Prince Tel: 509 1 22 6336/22 8858/22 7048
HONDURAS Ships inspection – Head office	Superintendencia de la Marina Mercante Fuerza Naval de Honduras Apartado Postal 1329 Comayaguela, DC
HONG KONG, CHINA As a flag Administration for PSC matters	Assistant Director of Marine Shipping Division Marine Department The Government of the Hong Kong Special Administrative Region 22/F., Harbour Building 38 Pier Road Central Hong Kong Tel: 852 2852 4404 Fax: 852 2854 9416 Email: km_varghese@mardep.gcn.gov.hk

AUTHORITY Competency	Competent Administration/Services Address
HONG KONG, **CHINA** Ships inspection – Head office	Assistant Director of Marine Shipping Division Marine Department The Government of the Hong Kong Special Administrative Region 22/F., Harbour Building 38 Pier Road Central Hong Kong Tel: 852 2852 4404 Fax: 852 2854 9416 Email: km_varghese@mardep.gcn.gov.hk

HUNGARY
Ships inspection –
Head office
	Superintendence for Shipping supervised by the
	  Ministry of Transport, Communication and
	  Waterways
	General Inspection for Transport
	H-1389 Budapest 62
	P.O. Box 102
	Tel: 36 1 111 7676 (main sb)
	          36 1 111 2261 (direct)
	Fax: 36 1 1111412

ICELAND As a flag State for PSC matters	Icelandic Maritime Administration Vesturvör 2 P.O. Box 120 IS-202 Kopavogur Tel: 354 560 0000 Fax: 354 560 0060 Email: skrifstofa@vh.is
Ships inspection – Head office	Icelandic Maritime Administration Vesturvör 2 P.O. Box 120 IS-202 Kopavogur Tel: 354 560 0000 Fax: 354 560 0060 Email: skrifstofa@vh.is

AUTHORITY Competency	Competent Administration/Services Address
INDIA As a flag State for PSC matters	"Jahaz Bhavan" Walchand Hirachand Marg Mumbai – 400001 Tel: 91 22 261 3651/52 Fax: 91 22 261 3655 Telex: 01186644 DGS IN Email: degeship@bom3.vsnl.net.in
Ships inspection – Head office	"Jahaz Bhavan" Walchand Hirachand Marg Mumbai – 400001 Tel: 91 22 261 3156/3651/3654/1788 Fax: 91 22 261 3655 Telex: 011 86644 DGS IN Email: degeship@bom3.vsnl.net.in
INDIAN OCEAN MOU MoU on PSC information – Manager	Information Manager South African Maritime Safety Authority (SAMSA) Private Bag X 7025 Roggebaai 8012 South Africa Tel: 27 21 4028980 Fax: 27 21 4216109 Email: samsaops@iafrica.com
MoU on PSC – Secretary	Head Land, Sada, Near Antarctic Study Centre Vasco da Gama Goa 403 804 India Tel: 91 832 52 0931 Fax: 91 832 52 0045 Email: iomou@goal.dot.net.in
INDONESIA Ships inspection – Head office	Director General of Sea Communications Ship Control & Inspections Jl. Medan Merdeka Barat No.8 Gedung Karsa Lantai 4 Jakarta Pusat 10110 Tel: 62 21 344 7310 Fax: 62 21 381 3269

AUTHORITY Competency	Competent Administration/Services Address
IRAN (ISLAMIC REPUBLIC OF) Ships inspection – Head office	Inspection Unit Bandar Shahid Rajai
IRAQ Ships inspection – Head office	Ministry of Transport and Communications P.O. Box 19199 Baghdad Telex: 2020 MOCBG IK
IRELAND Ships inspection – Head office	Maritime Safety and Environment Division The Secretary Department of the Marine Leeson Lane Dublin 2 Tel: 353 1 678 5444/678 5326/678 5341 Fax: 353 1 661 8214/661 3817/676 3616
ISRAEL Ships inspection – Head office	Director of Technical Services 102 Ha'atzmaut Street P.O. Box 33993 Haifa 33411 Tel: 972 4 8563160/8535416 Fax: 972 4 8514615/8510185
ITALY As a flag State for PSC matters	Direzione dei Servizi Sicurezza della Navigazione Servizio delle Ispezioni Ponte dei Mille 16100 Genova Tel: 39 010 241 2445 Fax: 39 010 241 2309
Ships inspection – Head office	Ministero dei Transporti e della Navigazione Comando Generale del Corpo delle Capitanerie di Porto Reparto VI – Ufficio I – Rapporti Internazionali Via dell'Arte 16 Roma EUR 00144 Tel: 39 06 5908 4551/39 06 5908 4211 39 06 5908 4819/39 06 5908 4719 39 06 5964 8256/39 06 5964 8173 Fax: 39 06 5964 8244/39 06 5922737 Email: sicnavi@libero.it

JAMAICA
Ships inspection –
Head office

Ministry of Public Utilities and Transport
2 St. Lucia Avenue
P.O. Box 9000
C.S.O.
Kingston 5
Tel: 001 876 929 2201
Fax: 001 876 754 7260
Email: rlee@jamaicaships.com

JAPAN
Ships inspection –
Head office

Inspection and Measurement Divison
Maritime Technology and Safety Bureau
Ministry of Transport
2-1-3 Kasumigaseki
Chiyoda-ku
Tokyo 100
Tel: 81 33 580 6398
Fax: 81 33 580 5047

JORDAN
Ships inspection –
Head office

Director General of the Ports Corporation
P.O. Box 115
Aqaba
Tel: 962 3 314031
Fax: 962 3 316204

KENYA
Ships inspection –
Head office

Ministry of Transport and Communications
The Permanent Secretary
c/o The High Commissioner
Kenya High Commission
45 Portland Place
London W1N 4AS
Tel: 44 20 7 636 2371/5
Fax: 44 20 7 323 6717
Telex: 262551

**KOREA
(DEMOCRATIC
PEOPLE'S
REPUBLIC OF)**
Ships inspection –
Head office

Maritime Administration Bureau of the
    Democratic People's Republic of Korea
Dongheungdong
Central District
Pyongyang
Tel: 00850 2 3816059
Fax: 00850 2 3814585

AUTHORITY Competency	Competent Administration/Services Address
KOREA **(REPUBLIC OF)** Ships inspection – Head office	Ship Inspection Division Director General Ministry of Maritime Affairs and Fisheries 139 Chungjong-No.3 Seodaemun-Gu Seoul 120-715 Tel: 822 3148 6323 Fax: 822 3148 6327 Email: ohkg@momaf.go.kr
KUWAIT Ships inspection – Head office	General Administration for Transport Affairs Ministry of Communications Director Marine Affairs Department P.O. Box 16 Safat Tel: 00965 4838230/4838231 Fax: 00965 4844831 Telex: US PTT KT 22197
LATVIA Ships inspection – Head office	Ministry of Transport Maritime Department Gogola iela 3 Riga LV 1003 Tel: 371 2 322 498 Fax: 371 7 331 406
LEBANON Ships inspection – Head office	Ministry of Transport Directorate General of Land and Maritime Transport Starco Bldg. 3rd Floor Beirut Tel: 961 1 371 644/371645 Fax: 961 1 371 647

AUTHORITY Competency	Competent Administration/Services Address
LIBERIA Ships inspection – Head office	Office of the Deputy Commissioner of Maritime Affairs of the Republic of Liberia Maritime Operations 8619 Westwood Center Drive Suite 300 Vienna VA 22182 United States Tel: 703 790 3434 Fax: 703 790 5655 Email: jpdeleo@liscr.com
LITHUANIA Ships inspection – Head office	Ministry of Transport of Lithuania Water Transport Department Gedimino pr. 17 LT-2679 Vilnius Tel: 370 2 393980 Fax: 370 2 393880 Email: ugniusl@transp.lt
MADAGASCAR Ships inspection – Head office	Ministère des Transports, de la Météorologie et du Tourisme B.P. 4139 Anosy Antananarivo Tel: 261 2 24604 Fax: 261 2 24001 Telex: MTMT MG 22301
MALAWI Ships inspection – Head office	The Secretary for Transport and Communications Marine Administration Private Bag 322 Capital City Lilongwe Tel: 265 783 066 Fax: 265 784 724
MALAYSIA Ships inspection – Head office	Marine Department Headquarters P.O. Box 12 42007 Port Klang Selangor Darul Ehsan Tel: 60 3 368 6616 60 3 254 8122 Fax: 60 3 255 7041

AUTHORITY Competency	Competent Administration/Services Address
MALDIVES Ships inspection – Head office	Ministry of Transport and Communications Huravee Building Ameeru Ahmed Magu Male Tel: 960 32 3991/3993 Fax: 960 32 3994 Telex: 77066 MOTS MF
MALTA Ships inspection – Head office	Malta Maritime Authority Merchant Shipping Directorate Maritime House Lascaris Wharf Valletta VLT 01 Tel: 356 250360 Fax: 356 241460
MARSHALL ISLANDS **(REPUBLIC OF THE)** Ships inspection – Head office	Marshall Islands Maritime & Corporate Administrators, Inc. c/o International Registries (UK) Ltd. Northumbrian House (2nd Floor) 14 Devonshire Square London EC2M 4TE Tel: 44 20 7 247 8782 Fax: 44 20 7 247 8771 Telex: (851) 25871 LIBSAF G
Ships inspection – Head office	Office of the Maritime Administrator Republic of the Marshall Islands Maritime Operations Department 11495 Commerce Park Drive Reston Virginia 20191-1507, USA Tel: 703 620 4880 Fax: 703 476 8522 Telex: 275501 IRI UR
MAURITANIA Ships inspection – Head office	Ministère des Pêches et de l'Economie Maritime Direction de la Marine Marchande B.P. 137 Ouakchott Tel: 2222 57893/52476-96 Fax: 2222 53146

AUTHORITY Competency	Competent Administration/Services Address

MAURITIUS
Ships inspection –
Head office
	Director of Shipping
	Ministry of Land Transport, Shipping and Port
	    Development
	New Government Centre
	Port Louis
	Tel: 230 201 2115
	              230 201 1272
	Fax: 230 201 3417

MEDITERRANEAN MOU MoU on PSC	Direction de la Marine Marchande Bd. Felix Houphouet Boigny Casablanca Morocco Tel: 212 2 278092/276010 Fax: 212 2 273340 Email: marine@maroconline.com
MoU on PSC – Secretary	27 Admiral Hamza Pasha Street Roushdy Alexandria Egypt Tel: 203 544 6538 Fax: 203 546 6360
MEXICO Ships inspection – Head office	Coordinacion General de Puertos Dirección General de Marina Mercante Secretaria de Communicaciones y Transportes Municipio Libel No 377 piso 8 Ala B Col. Sta. Cruz Atoyac C. P. 03310 Tel: 688 72 13/688 00 03 Fax: 604 38 89/605 83 21
MONACO Ships inspection – Head office	Directeur des Affaires maritimes Service de la Marine 6, Quai Antoine 1er MC-98000 Monaco Tel: 377 93 15 86 78 Fax: 377 93 15 37 15 Email: ontarensky@gouv.mc

AUTHORITY Competency	Competent Administration/Services Address
MOROCCO Ships inspection – Head office	Ministère des Pêches maritimes et de la Marine Marchande Direction de la Marine Marchande Cité Administrative Agdal Rabat Tel: 212 7 77 1075/77 1061 Fax: 212 7 77 273340/77 8540
MOZAMBIQUE Ships inspection – Head office	SAFMAR Av. Marquês de Pombal, 279 Caixa Postal 4317 Maputo Tel: 258 1 420552 Fax: 258 1 424007
NAMIBIA Ships inspection – Head office	Ministry of Works, Transport and Communication Directorate of Maritime Affairs Private Bag 5004 Walvis Bay Tel: 264 61 208 2195 Fax: 264 61 228 560
NETHERLANDS As a flag State for PSC matters	Netherlands Shipping Inspectorate P.O. Box 8634 3000 AP Rotterdam Tel: 31 10 266 8500 Fax: 31 10 202 3520
Ships inspection – Head office	Netherlands Shipping Inspectorate P.O. Box 8634 3000 AP Rotterdam Tel: 31 10 266 8500 Fax: 31 10 202 3424
NETHERLANDS ANTILLES Ships inspection – Head office	Shipping Inspectorate Pletterijweg Z/N Parera Willemstad Curaçao Tel: 599 9612 361 Fax: 599 9612 964

AUTHORITY Competency	Competent Administration/Services Address
NEW ZEALAND Ships inspection – Head office	Maritime Safety Authority Level 8 AMP House 109 Featherston Street P.O. Box 27006 Wellington Tel: 64 4 473 0111 (mobile – 64 25 426 344) Fax: 64 4 473 6699/8111
NIGERIA Ships inspection – Head office	Ministry of Transport Director Maritime Services Federal Secretariat 2nd Floor, Annex III Shehu Shagari Way Maitama Abuja Tel: 09 523 6094/523 7050 Fax: 09 523 7050
NORWAY Ships inspection – Head office	Norwegian Maritime Directorate Inspection Department Stensberggt. 27 P.O. Box 8123 DEP N-0032 Oslo Tel: 47 22 45 45 00/31 Fax: 47 22 56 79 74 Telex: 067+21557 SDIR N Email: norvald.moltubakk@sjofartsdir.dep.no
OMAN Ships inspection – Head office	Ministry of Communications, Maritime and Seaport Affairs P.O. Box 684 PC 113 Muscat Tel: 968 780099 Fax: 968 702044 Telex: 3390 MWASALAT ON Email: dgpma@gto.net.om

AUTHORITY Competency	Competent Administration/Services Address
PAKISTAN As a flag State for PSC matters	Ministry of Communications Ports & Shipping Wing Plot No. 12 Misc. Area Mai Kolachi Bypass Karachi-74200 Tel: 092 21 9206405/6 Fax: 092 21 9206407/9204191 Telex: 29822 DGPS PK Email: sa568@aol.net.pk
Ships inspection – Head office	Ministry of Communications Ports & Shipping Wing Plot No. 12 Misc. Area Mai Kolachi Bypass Karachi-74200 Tel: 092 21 9206405/6 Fax: 092 21 9206407/9204191 Telex: 29822 DGPS PK Email: sa568@aol.net.pk
PALESTINIAN NATIONAL AUTHORITY Ships inspection – Head office	Ministry of Transport Director of Maritime Affairs Department Palestinian National Authority P.O. Box 5202 Gaza Tel: 972 7 2829133 972 7 2863322 Fax: 972 7 2822297 972 7 2825265
PANAMA Ships inspection – Head office	Directorate General of Consular and Maritime Affairs Secnaves 50th Street & 69th Street Plaza Guadelupe San Francisco P.O. Box 5245 Panama 5 Tel: 507 270 0166/270 03 26 (Director) 507 270 0277 Fax: 507 270 0716/270 0039 Email: pregistry@pan.gbm.net

AUTHORITY Competency	Competent Administration/Services Address
PANAMA Ships inspection – Head office	Department of Maritime Safety Directorate of Consular and Maritime Affairs 6 West 48th Street 10th Floor New York 10036 USA Tel: 212 869 6440 Fax: 212 575 2285/575 2288 Telex: 238185 Email: Segumar@Tiac.Net
PAPUA NEW GUINEA Ships inspection – Head office	The Secretary Department of Transport P.O. Box 457 Konedobu National Capital District Tel: 675 22 2532 Fax: 675 21 7310 Telex: NE 22203
PARAGUAY Ships inspection – Head office	Ministerio de Obras Públicas y Comunicaciones Dirección General de la Marina Mercante Oliva y Alberdi Asunción
PARIS MOU MoU on PSC information – Manager	Centre Administratif des Affaires Maritimes (CAAM) 27 Quai Solidor B.P. 130 35408 Saint-Malo Cedex France Tel: 33 02 99 19 60 00 Fax: 33 02 99 82 78 93 Email: jacques.benard@equipement.gouv.fr benoit.faist@wanadoo.fr

AUTHORITY Competency	Competent Administration/Services Address

PARIS MOU
MoU on PSC – Secretary

Secretariat
Paris MOU on Port State Control
Artillery Building
Nieuwe Uitleg 1
2514 BP
The Hague
PO Box 20904
2500 EX
The Hague
The Netherlands
Tel: 31 70 351 1508
Fax: 31 70 351 1599
Email: office@parismou.org
        Richard.Schiferli@parismou.org
        www.parismou.organization

PERU
Ships inspection –
Head office

Dirección General de Capitinías y Guardacostas
Dirección de Control de Intereses Acuáticos
Constitución 150
Callao
Tel: 51 14 4296536
Fax: 51 14 4296536
Email: dicacont@marina.mil.pe

PHILIPPINES
Ships inspection –
Head office

Philippine Coast Guard
25th Street
Port Area
Manila
Tel: 63 2 40 0290

POLAND
Ships inspection –
Head office

Ministry of Transport and Maritime Economy
Department of Maritime and Inland Waters
Administration
Ul. Chalubinskiego 4/6
00-928 Warszawa
Tel: 48 2262 11448/48 2262 19437
Fax: 48 2262 88515
Telex: 96+813 614 PKP PL

AUTHORITY Competency	Competent Administration/Services Address

PORTUGAL
As a flag State for
PSC matters

Edificio Vasco da Gama
Alcandara-Mar
1300 Lisboa
Tel: 351 1 397 9821
Fax: 351 1 397 9794

Ships inspection –
Head office

Direçäo-General de Marinha
Praça do Comércio
1188 Lisboa Codex
Tel: 351 1 34 70 63 6
Fax: 351 1 34 24 13 7
Telex: 96+4044 3536 DIRMAR P

QATAR
Ships inspection –
Head office

Ministry of Communications and Transport
The Director
Ports Department
P.O. Box 313
Doha
Tel: 974 457 457
Fax: 974 413 563
Telex: 4378DH

ROMANIA
Ships inspection –
Head office

State Inspectorate for Civil Navigation Ministry
   of Transport
Bd. Dinicu Golescu 38
Section 1
77113 Bucharest
Tel: 40 1 6141506/6157704
Fax: 40 1 3122528

RUSSIAN FEDERATION
Ships inspection –
Head office

Head office of Administration Central State
   Maritime Inspection on Safety of Navigation
Federal Maritime Administration of Russia
Department of Maritime Transport
103759 Moscow
Rozhdestvenka Str 1/4
Tel: 7 095 926 1121
Fax: 7 095 926 9128

AUTHORITY Competency	Competent Administration/Services Address
SAINT KITTS **AND NEVIS** Ships inspection – Head office	Sea Port Authority Sea Port Manager Bird Rock Bassatere Tel: 809 465 8109/8121 Fax: 809 465 8124
SAINT LUCIA Ships inspection – Head office	Sea Ports Authority Chief Pilot P.O. Box 651 Castries Tel: 809 452 7508/2893 Fax: 809 452 2062
SAINT VINCENT **AND THE GRENADINES** Ships inspection – Head office	The Commissioner for Maritime Affairs of Saint Vincent and the Grenadines 8 Avenue de Frontenex CH–1207 Geneva Switzerland Tel: 41 22 7076300 Fax: 41 22 7076350 Telex: 421925
Ships inspection – Head office	The Deputy Commissioner for Maritime Affairs of Saint Vincent and the Grenadines Monaco Office 74 Bd D'italie E/F MC 98000 Monaco Tel: 377 93 104450 Fax: 377 93 104499 Telex: 489171 SVGReg
SAUDI ARABIA Ships inspection – Head office	Ministry of Communications Deputy Minister of Communications for Transport Affairs Marine Department Riyadh 11178 Tel: 966 1 4021588 Fax: 966 1 4021584

AUTHORITY Competency	Competent Administration/Services Address

SENEGAL
Ships inspection –
Head office
	Ministère de l'Equipement
	Direction de la Marine Marchande
	B.P. 4032
	Dakar
	Tel: 221 821 3643
	            221 823 6862
	Fax: 221 822 6284
	            221 823 8720

SEYCHELLES Ships inspection – Head office	Ministry of Tourism and Transport Principal Secretary Department of Transport P.O. Box 47 Mahé Tel: 248 24701 Fax: 248 24004
SIERRA LEONE Ships inspection – Head office	The Permanent Secretary Department of Transport and Communications Ministerial Building George Street Freetown Tel: 232 22 223202 Fax: 232 22 228488
SINGAPORE Ships inspection – Head office	Director of Marine Maritime and Port Authority of Singapore 21-00 PSA Building 460 Alexandra Road Singapore 119963 Tel: 65 375 1600 Fax: 65 375 6231 Email: shipping@mpa.gov.sg
SLOVAKIA Ships inspection – Head office	Ministerstvo dopravy, pôst a telekomunikácii Odbor vodnej dopravy Namestie Slobody 6 P.O. Box 100 810 05 Bratislava Tel: 42 7 256 486 Fax: 42 7 256 486

AUTHORITY Competency	Competent Administration/Services Address
SLOVENIA Ships inspection – Head office	Ministry of Transport and Communications Slovenian Maritime Directorate of the Republic of Slovenia Ukmarjev trg 2 6000 Koper Tel: 386 66 271 216 Fax: 386 66 271 447 Telex: 34 235 UP POM SI Email: ivo.maraspin@gov.si
SOLOMON ISLANDS Ships inspection – Head office	Ministry of Transport, Works & Utilities P.O. Box G32 Honiara Tel: 677 22510 Fax: 677 23798

SOUTH AFRICA
Ships inspection –
Head office
	National Operations Manager
	South African Maritime Safety Authority
	   (SAMSA)
	Private Bag X 7025
	Roggebaai 8012
	Tel: 027 21 4028980
	Fax: 027 21 4216109
	Email: brwatt@iafrica.com
	          samsaops@iafrica.com

SPAIN Ships inspection – Head office	Inspección General Marítima Dirección General de la Marina Mercante Calle Ruiz de Alarcón 1 28071 Madrid Tel: 34 91 597 9258/9247 Fax: 34 91 597 9003/34 91 597 9235 Telex: 062+44874 MAMER E 062+27298 MAMER E
SRI LANKA Ships inspection – Head office	Ministry of Ports and Shipping Director of Merchant Shipping 45 Leyden Bastian Road Colombo 1 Tel: 94 1 435160

AUTHORITY Competency	Competent Administration/Services Address
SUDAN Ships inspection – Head office	Maritime Administration Directorate Box 2534 Khartoum Tel: 249 79343/79114 Fax: 249 11 79349
SURINAME Ships inspection – Head office	Ministry of Transport, Trade and Industry Permanent Secretary of Transport Kleine Waterstraat No. 4 Paramaribo Tel: 597 75080
SWEDEN Ships inspection – Head office	Swedish Maritime Administration Maritime Safety Inspectorate SE-601 78 Norrkoping Tel: 46 11 19 10 00 Fax: 46 11 23 99 34/46 11 10 19 49 Telex: 084+64380 SHIPADM S Email: inspektion@shipadm.se
SWITZERLAND Ships inspection – Head office	Swiss Maritime Navigation Office Postfach Nauenstrasse 49 Basel 4002 Tel: 41 61 270 91 20 Fax: 41 61 270 91 29
SYRIAN ARAB REPUBLIC Ships inspection – Head office	Ministry of Transport General Directorate of Ports Lattakia Syria P.O. Box 505 Tel: 00963 41 472593/472597/471577/ 473876/473333 Fax: 00963 41 475805 Telex: 451216 MWANI SY
TANZANIA (UNITED REPUBLIC OF) Ships inspection – Head office	Ministry of Communications and Transport The Principal Secretary P.O. Box 9144 Dar es Salaam Tel: 255 51 112858 Fax: 255 51 112751

AUTHORITY Competency	Competent Administration/Services Address
THAILAND Ships inspection – Head office	Harbour Department Ministry of Transport and Communications Ratchadamnoon Nok Avenue Bangkok Tel: 66 2 2813422 Fax: 66 2 2801714 Telex: 7000 MINOCOM TH
THE FORMER **YUGOSLAV REPUBLIC** **OF MACEDONIA** Ships inspection – Head office	Ministry of Transport and Communications Llindenska bb 91000 Skopje Tel: 389 91 119 378 Fax: 389 91 114 258

TOGO
Ships inspection –
Head office
	Marine Ship Surveyor, Ministère des Mines,
	    de l'Equipement, des Transports et
	    des Postes et Télécommunications
	Direction des Affaires Maritimes
	PO Box 4771
	Lomé
	Tel: 228 274 742
	Fax: 228 270 248/272 627
	Email: aeroportint.lome.tokoin

TONGA Ships inspection – Head office	Ministry of Marine and Ports P.O Box 397 Nuku'alofa Tel: 676 22 555/26 233 Fax: 676 26 234 Email: marine@kalianet.to
TRINIDAD AND **TOBAGO** Ships inspection – Head office	Ministry of Works and Transport Director of Maritime Services P.O. Box 493 Port of Spain Tel: 809 625 3858/3218/7004 Fax: 809 624 5884

AUTHORITY Competency	Competent Administration/Services Address
TUNISIA Ships inspection – Head office	Office de la Marine Marchande et des Ports Bâtiment administratif 2060 La Goulette Tel: 216 735 300 Fax: 216 735 812 Email: OMMP@Email.ati.tn
TURKEY Ships inspection – Head office	Prime Ministry Undersecretariat for Maritime Affairs General Directorate for Maritime Transport Anit Caddesi No. 8 (06580) Tandogan Ankara Tel: 312 212 8061/8790 Fax: 312 212 8278

UKRAINE
Ships inspection –
Head office
	Ministry of Transport of Ukraine
	State Administration of Merchant Marine
	   and River Transport of Ukraine
	Shipping Safety Inspectorate of Ukraine
	29 Shevchenko Ave.
	270058 Odessa
	Tel: 380 482 42 80 60/482 68 27 84/
	        482 42 82 01
	Fax: 380 482 42 80 73/68 54 36
	Email: maradmin@odtel.net
	        www.flotinspection.uptel.net

UNITED ARAB EMIRATES Ships inspection – Head office	Ministry of Communications The Under-Secretary P.O. Box 900 Abu Dhabi Tel: 971 2 662903/2 662904 Fax: 971 2 664422 Telex: 22668 COMSAD EM

AUTHORITY Competency	Competent Administration/Services Address

UNITED KINGDOM
Ships inspection –
Head office
	Maritime and Coastguard Agency
	Marine Directorate
	Spring Place
	105 Commerical Road
	Southampton SO15 1EG
	Tel: Policy: 44 23 80 329 211
	       Operations: 44 23 80 329 215
	Fax: 44 23 80 329 251
	       44 23 80 329 104
	Email: alan_cubbin@mcga.gov.uk
	      paul_owen@mcga.gov.uk
	      www.mcagency.org.uk

UNITED KINGDOM (ANGUILLA) Ships inspection – Head office	Office of Superintendent of Ports, Harbours & Piers Road Bay Anguilla British West Indies Tel: 264 497 3467 Fax: 264 497 5258
UNITED KINGDOM (BERMUDA) Ships inspection – Head office	Bermuda Registry of Shipping P.O. Box HM 1628 Hamilton HM GX Bermuda Tel: 441 295 7251 Fax: 441 295 3718/5713
UNITED KINGDOM (CAYMAN ISLANDS) Ships inspection – Head office	Cayman Islands Shipping Registry Elizabethan Square Phase Four – Third Floor (PO Box GT 2256) George Town Grand Cayman British West Indies Tel: 345 949 8831 Fax: 345 949 8849

AUTHORITY Competency	Competent Administration/Services Address
UNITED KINGDOM (GIBRALTAR) Ships inspection – Head office	Registry of Ships Duke of Kent House Cathedral Square Gibraltar Tel: 350 77254 Fax: 350 77011
UNITED KINGDOM (ISLE OF MAN) Ships inspection – Head office	Marine Administration Peregrine House Peel Road Douglas Isle of Man British Isles IM1 5EH Tel: 44 1624 688500 Fax: 44 1624 688501
UNITED KINGDOM (TURKS AND CAICOS ISLANDS) Ships inspection – Head office	Government House Grand Turk Turks and Caicos Islands British West Indies Tel: 809 946 2801/2807 Fax: 809 946 1120
UNITED KINGDOM (VIRGIN ISLANDS) Ships inspection – Head office	Registrar of Shipping Financial Services Department Haycraft Building Pasea Estate Tortola British Virgin Islands Tel: 284 494 4190/6430/4381 Fax: 284 494 5016
UNITED STATES Ships inspection – Head office	U.S. Coast Guard Headquarters Assistant Commandant for Merchant Marine Safety and Environmental Protection (GM) 2100 Second Street S.W. Washington D.C. 20593-0001 Tel: 1 202 267 2200 Fax: 1 202 267 4839 Telex: 64+089 2427 COASTGUARD WSH

AUTHORITY Competency	Competent Administration/Services Address

URUGUAY
As a flag State for
PSC matters

Registral y de Marina Mercante
Rbla 25 de Agosto de 1825
Comando de la Armada Building 1st Floor
Montevideo
Tel: 589 2 964914
Fax: 589 2 964914
Telex: 032 22557 ARMADA UY

Ships inspection –
Head office

Prefectura de Trouville
Registral y de Marina Mercante
Rbla 25 de Agosto de 1825
Comando de la Armada Building 1st Floor
Montevideo
Tel: 598 2 964914
Fax: 598 2 964914

VANUATU
As a flag State for
PSC matters

Deputy Commissioner of Maritime Affairs
Vanuatu Maritime Services Limited
42 Broadway
Suite 1200-18
New York
N.Y.10004
United States
Tel: 1 212 425 9600
Fax: 1 212 425 9652
Email: vmsnyc@attglobal.net

Ships inspection –
Head office

The Commissioner of Maritime Affairs
Vanuatu Maritime Authority
Marine Quay
Private Mailbag 32
Port Vila
Tel: 678 23128
Fax: 678 22949
Email: vma@vanuatu.com.vu

AUTHORITY Competency	Competent Administration/Services Address
VENEZUELA Ships inspection – Head office	Ministerio de Transporte y Comunicaciones Director General Sectorial de Transporte Acuático Torre Este del Parque Central Piso 38 Caracas Tel: 58 2 332 28 91 Telex: 29692 MTCVCNO Email: cguard@truevision.net
VIETNAM Ships inspection – Head office	Vietnam National Maritime Bureau 7A Lang Ha Street Hanoi Tel: 844 351 284/350 370 Fax: 844 350 729
VIÑA DEL MAR AGREEMENT Ships inspection – Head office	Viña del Mar Agreement Secretariat Prefectura Naval Argentina Av. Eduardo Madero 235 Buenos Aires 1106 Argentina Tel: 54 11 4318 7475 Fax: 54 11 4318 7643 Telex: 18581 PREFEC AR Email: ciala@sudnet.com.ar

**WEST AND CENTRAL
AFRICAN MOU**
MoU on PSC information –
Manager
	Maritime Organisation for West and Central Africa
	  (MOWCA)
	B.P V257
	Abidjan
	Côte d'Ivoire
	Tel: 225 20217115/225 20223193
	Fax: 225 20224532/225 20233197
	        225 20227493/
	Email: mowca@africaonline.co.cl

MoU on PSC – Secretary	Secretariat of the West and Central African MOU c/o National Maritime Authority 4 Burma Road Apapa Lagos Nigeria Tel: 58 72214/58 74884/58 71673/ 58 75730/26 94624 Fax: 58 71329 Email: boluwole@hotmail.com

AUTHORITY Competency	Competent Administration/Services Address
YEMEN Ships inspection – Head office	Public Corporation for Maritime Affairs The Chairman P.O. Box 19395 Sanaa Tel: 969 967 1 414412 Fax: 969 967 1 414645

Notes

Notes

Notes

Notes

Notes

Notes

Notes

Notes

Notes

Notes